glencoe
teenhealth
safety + a healthy environment

D0841799

McGraw Hill Education

Bothell, WA • Chicago, IL • Columbus, OH • New York, NY

Meet the Authors

Mary H. Bronson, Ph.D. recently retired after teaching for 30 years in Texas public schools. Dr. Bronson taught health education in grades K–12 as well as health education methods classes at the graduate and undergraduate levels. As Health Education Specialist for the Dallas School District, Dr. Bronson developed and implemented a district-wide health eduation program. She has been honored as Texas Health Educator of the Year by the Texas Association for Health, Physical Education, Recreation, and Dance and selected Teacher of the Year twice by her colleagues. Dr. Bronson has assisted school districts throughout the country in developing local health education programs. She is also the coauthor of Glencoe Health.

Michael J. Cleary, Ed.D., C.H.E.S. is a professor at Slippery Rock University, where he teaches methods courses and supervises field experiences. Dr. Cleary taught health education at Evanston Township High School in Illinois and later served as the Lead Teacher Specialist at the McMillen Center for Health Education in Fort Wayne, Indiana. Dr. Cleary has published widely on curriculum development and assessment in K–12 and college health education. Dr. Cleary is also coauthor of Glencoe Health.

Betty M. Hubbard, Ed.D., C.H.E.S. has taught science and health education in grades 6–12 as well as undergraduate- and graduate-level courses. She is a professor at the University of Central Arkansas, where in addition to teaching she conducts in-service training for health education teachers in school districts throughout Arkansas. In 1991, Dr. Hubbard received the university's teaching excellence award. Her publications, grants, and presentations focus on research-based, comprehensive health instruction. Dr. Hubbard is a fellow of the American Association for Health Education and serves as the contributing editor of the Teaching Ideas feature of the American Journal of Health Education.

Contributing Author

Dinah Zike, M.Ed. is an international curriculum consultant and inventor who has designed and developed educational products and three-dimensional, interactive graphic organizers for more than 35 years. As president and founder of Dinah-Might Adventures, L.P., Dinah is author of more than 100 award-winning educational publications. Dinah has a B.S. and an M.S. in educational curriculum and instruction from Texas A&M University. Dinah Zike's Foldables® are an exclusive feature of McGraw-Hill.

MHEonline.com

Copyright © 2014 by McGraw-Hill Education

Send all inquiries to:
McGraw-Hill Education
STEM Learning Solutions Center
8787 Orion Place
Columbus, OH 43240

ISBN: 978-0-07-664047-8
MHID: 0-07-664047-7

Printed in the United States of America.

5 6 7 8 9 10 QVS 20 19 18 17 16

STEM McGraw-Hill is committed to providing instructional materials in Science, Technology, Engineering, and Mathematics (STEM) that give all students a solid foundation, one that prepares them for college and careers in the 21st century.

Reviewers

Professional Reviewers

Amy Eyler, Ph.D., CHES
Washington University in St. Louis
St. Louis, Missouri

Shonali Saha, M.D.
Johns Hopkins School of Medicine
Baltimore, Maryland

Roberta Duyff
Duyff & Associates
St. Louis, MO

Teacher Reviewers

Lou Ann Donlan
Altoona Area School District
Altoona, PA

Steve Federman
Loveland Intermediate School
Loveland, Ohio

Rick R. Gough
Ashland Middle School
Ashland, Ohio

Jacob Graham
Oblock Junior High
Plum, Pennsylvania

William T. Gunther
Clarkston Community Schools
Clarkston, MI

Ellie Hancock
Somerset Area School District
Somerset, PA

Diane Hursky
Independence Middle School
Bethel Park, PA

Veronique Javier
Thomas Cardoza Middle School
Jackson, Mississippi

Patricia A. Landon
Patrick F. Healy Middle School
East Orange, NJ

Elizabeth Potash
Council Rock High School South
Holland, PA

The Path to Good Health

Your health book has many features that will aid you in your learning. Some of these features are listed below. You can use the map at the right to help you find these and other special features in the book.

✳ The **Big Idea** can be found at the start of each lesson.

✳ Your **Foldables**® help you organize your notes.

✳ The **Quick Write** at the start of each lesson will help you think about the topic and give you an opportunity to write about it in your journal.

✳ The **Bilingual Glossary** contains vocabulary terms and definitions in Spanish and English.

✳ **Health Skills Activities** help you learn more about each of the 10 health skills.

✳ **Infographs** provide a colorful, visual way to learn about current health news and trends.

✳ The **Fitness Zone** provides an online fitness resource that includes podcasts, videos, activity cards, and more!

✳ **Hands-On Health Activities** give you the opportunity to complete hands-on projects.

✳ **Videos** encourage you to explore real life health topics.

✳ **Audio** directs you to online audio chapter summaries.

✳ **Web Quest** activities challenge you to relate lesson concepts to current health news and research.

✳ **Review** your understanding of health concepts with lesson reviews and quizzes.

What's the word on the street? The **glossary** lists vocabulary terms in English and Spanish.

Quick! Write about your good health habits using a **Quick Write** activity.

Think big! Start your journey with a **Big Idea** and increase your pace with **Foldables**®.

Sharpen your skills with **Health Skills Activities**.

Got a nose for news? Check out each chapter's **infographs** for health news and trends.

Get into the zone –the **Fitness Zone!** Listen to podcasts, watch videos, and more.

Show what you know by completing a **Hands-On Health Activity**.

Stop! Look and Listen! Watch a Health eSpotlight **video** and explore real life health topics. Listen to the **audio** summaries to review the chapter.

Go on a quest. Take a **Web Quest** to learn more about health news and research.

Finish strong! **Review** your understanding of health concepts with lesson reviews and quizzes.

Contents

F4F-1 through F4F-9
Flip your book over to see a special section on fitness.

chapter 1

Safety

Your Total Health

WHAT IS HEALTH?

Do you know someone you would describe as "healthy"? What kinds of traits do they have? Maybe they are involved in sports. Maybe they just "look" healthy. Looking fit and feeling well are important, but there is more to having good health. Good health also includes getting along well with others and feeling good about yourself.

Your physical, emotional, and social health are all related and make up your total health.

Health, the *combination of physical, mental/emotional, and social well-being,* may look like the sides of a triangle. You need all three sides to make the triangle. Each side supports the other two sides. Your physical health, mental/emotional health, and social health are all related and make up your total health.

Physical Health

Physical health is one side of the health triangle. Engaging in physical activity every day will help to build and maintain your physical health. Some of the ways you can improve your physical health include the following:

❀ Choose nutritious meals and snacks.

❀ Get regular checkups from a doctor and a dentist.

❀ Shower or bathe each day. Brush and floss your teeth at least twice every day.

❀ When playing sports, using protective gear and following safety rules will help you avoid injuries.

❀ Most teens need about nine hours of sleep every night.

You can also have good physical health by avoiding harmful behaviors, such as using alcohol, tobacco, and other drugs. The use of tobacco has been linked to many diseases, such as heart disease and cancer.

Mental/Emotional Health

Another side of the health triangle is your mental/emotional health. How do you handle your feelings, thoughts, and emotions each day? You can improve your mental/emotional health by talking and thinking about yourself in a healthful way. Share your thoughts and feelings with your family, a trusted adult, or with a friend.

If you are mentally and emotionally healthy, you can face challenges in a positive way. Be patient with yourself when you try to learn new subjects or new skills. Remember that everybody makes mistakes—including you! Next time you can do better.

Taking action to reach your goals is another way to develop good mental/emotional health. This can help you focus your energy and give you a sense of accomplishment. Make healthful choices, keep your promises, and take responsibility for what you do, and you will feel good about yourself and your life.

Social Health

A third side of the health triangle is your social health. Social health means how you relate to people at home, at school, and everywhere in your world. Strong friendships and family relationships are signs of good social health.

Do you get along well with your friends, classmates, and teachers? Do you spend time with your family? You can develop skills for having good relationships. Good social health includes supporting the people you care about. It also includes communicating with, respecting, and valuing people. Sometimes you may disagree with others. You can disagree and express your thoughts, but be thoughtful and choose your words carefully.

Your total health is made up of three parts, like a triangle.

MENTAL/EMOTIONAL HEALTH

YOUR TOTAL HEALTH is a combination of physical, mental/emotional, and social health.

PHYSICAL HEALTH

SOCIAL HEALTH

ACHIEVING WELLNESS

What is the difference between health and wellness? Wellness is *a state of well-being or balanced health over a long period of time.* Your health changes from day to day. One day you may feel tired if you did not get enough sleep. Maybe you worked very hard at sports practice. The next day, you might feel well rested and full of energy because you rested. Your emotions also change. You might feel sad one day but happy the next day.

Your overall health is like a snapshot of your physical, mental/emotional, and social health. Your wellness takes a longer view. Being healthy means balancing the three sides of your health triangle over weeks or months. Wellness is sometimes represented by a continuum, or scale, that gives a picture of your health at a certain time. It may also tell you how well you are taking care of yourself.

The Mind-Body Connection

Your emotions have a lot to do with your physical health. Think about an event in your own life that made you feel sad. How did you deal with this emotion? Sometimes people have a difficult time dealing with their emotions. This can have a negative effect on their physical health. For example, they might get headaches, backaches, upset stomachs, colds, the flu, or even more serious diseases. Why do you think this happens?

Your mind and body connect through your nervous system. This system includes thousands of miles of nerves. The nerves link your brain to your body. Upsetting thoughts and feelings sometimes affect the signals from your brain to other parts of your body.

Your **emotions** have *a lot* to do with *your* **physical health.**

The mind-body connection describes *how your emotions affect your physical and overall health and how your overall health affects your emotions.* This connection shows again how important it is to keep the three sides of the health triangle balanced. If you become very sad or angry, or if you have other strong emotions, talk to someone. Sometimes talking to a good friend helps. Sometimes you may need the services of a counselor or a medical professional.

The Wellness Scale identifies how healthy you are at a given point in time.

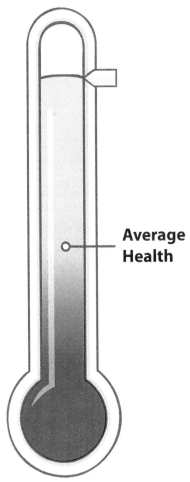

Peak Health

Practices good habits and behaviors; stays informed

Practices unhealthy habits and behaviors; lacks up-to-date information

Average Health

Poor Health

Health Influences _and_ Risk Factors

WHAT INFLUENCES YOUR HEALTH?

What are your favorite foods or activities? Your answers reflect your personal tastes, or likes and dislikes. Your health is influenced by your personal tastes and by many other factors such as:

- heredity
- environment
- family and friends
- culture
- media
- attitudes
- behavior

Heredity

You can control some of these factors, but not all of them. For example, you cannot control the natural color of your hair or eyes. Heredity (huh•RED•i•tee) is _the passing of traits from parents to their biological children._ Heredity determines the color of your eyes and hair, and other physical traits, or parts of your appearance. Genes are the basic units of heredity. They are made from chemicals called DNA, and they create the pattern for your physical traits. You inherited, or received, half of your DNA from your mother and half from your father.

Traits such as eye and hair color are inherited from parents.

Environment

Think about where you live. Do you live in a city, a suburb, a small town, or in a rural area? Where you live is the physical part of your environment (en•VY•ruhn•mehnt), or _all the living and nonliving things around you._

Environment is another factor that affects your personal health. Your physical environment includes the home you live in, the school you attend, and the air and water around you.

Your _social environment_ includes the people in your life. They can be friends, classmates, and neighbors. Your friends and peers, or _people close to you in age who are a lot like you,_ may influence your choices.

You may feel pressure to think and act like them. Peer pressure can also influence health choices. The influence can be positive or negative. Helping a friend with homework, volunteering with a friend, or simply listening to a friend are examples of positive peer influence. A friend who wants you to drink alcohol, for example, is a negative influence. Recreation is also a part of your social environment. Playing games and enjoying physical activities with others can have a positive effect on your health.

Culture

Your family is one of the biggest influences on your life. It shapes your cultural background, or *the beliefs, customs, and traditions of a specific group of people.* You learned that your family influences your health. In addition to your family, your culture, or *the collected beliefs, customs, and behaviors of a group,* also affects your health. Your family and their culture may influence the foods you eat as well as the activities and special events you celebrate with special foods. Some families fast (do not eat food) during religious events. Ahmed's family observes the holiday of Ramadan.

During this holiday, members of his family fast until sundown. Your family might also celebrate traditions that include dances, foods, ceremonies, songs, and games. Your culture can also affect your health. Knowing how your lifestyle and family history relate to health problems can help you stay well.

Media

What do television, radio, movies, magazines, newspapers, books, billboards, and the Internet have in common? They are all forms of media, or *various methods for communicating information.* The media is another factor that affects your personal health.

The media provide powerful sources of information and influence.

You may learn helpful new facts about health on the Internet or television. You might also see a commercial for the latest video game or athletic shoes. The goal of commercials on television or the Internet, as well as advertisements in print, is to make you want to buy a product. The product may be good or bad for your health. You can make wise health choices by learning to evaluate, or *determine the quality* of everything you see, hear, or read.

The celebration of Kwanzaa is a tradition in many African American families.

YOUR BEHAVIOR AND YOUR HEALTH

Do you protect your skin from the sun? Do you get enough sleep so that you are not tired during the day? Do you eat healthful foods? Do you listen to a friend who needs to talk about a problem? Your answers to these questions reflect your personal **lifestyle factors,** or *the behaviors and habits that help determine a person's level of health.* Positive lifestyle factors promote good health. Negative lifestyle factors promote poor health.

Positive lifestyle factors promote **good** *health.*

Your **attitude,** or your *feelings and beliefs,* toward your personal lifestyle factors plays an important role in your health. You will also have greater success in managing your health if you keep a positive attitude. Teens who have a positive attitude about their health are more likely to practice good health habits and take responsibility for their health.

Risk Behaviors

"Dangerous intersection. Proceed with caution." "Don't walk." "No lifeguard on duty." You have probably seen these signs or similar signs. They are posted to warn you about possible risks or dangers and to keep you safe.

 Eating well-balanced meals, starting with a good breakfast.

 Getting at least 60 minutes of physical activity daily.

 Sleeping at least eight hours every night.

 Doing your best in school and other activities.

 Avoiding tobacco, alcohol, and other drugs.

 Following safety rules and wearing protective gear.

 Relating well to family, friends, and classmates.

Lifestyle factors affect your personal health.

Risk, or *the chance that something harmful may happen to your health and wellness,* is part of everyday life. Some risks are easy to identify. Everyday tasks such as preparing food with a knife or crossing a busy street both carry some risk. Other risks are more hidden. Some foods you like might be high in fat.

You cannot avoid every kind of risk. However, the risks you can avoid often involve risk behavior. A risk behavior is an action or behavior that might cause injury or harm to you or others. Playing a sport can be risky, but if you wear protective gear, you may avoid injury. Wear a helmet when you ride a bike to avoid the risk of a head injury if you fall. Smoking cigarettes is another risk behavior that you can avoid. Riding in a car without a safety belt is a risk behavior you can avoid by buckling up. Another risk behavior is having a lifestyle with little physical activity, such as sitting in front of the TV or a computer instead of being active. You can avoid many kinds of risk by taking responsibility for your personal health behaviors and avoiding risk.

RISKS AND CONSEQUENCES

All risk behaviors have consequences. Some consequences are minor or short-term. You might eat a sweet snack just before dinner so that you lose your appetite for a healthy meal. Other risk behaviors may have serious or life-threatening consequences. These are long-term consequences.

Experimenting with alcohol, tobacco, or other drugs has long-term consequences that can seriously damage your health. They can affect all three sides of your health triangle. They can lead to dangerous addictions, which are physical and mental dependencies.

These substances can confuse the user's judgment and can increase the risks he or she takes. Using these substances may also lead to problems with family and friends, and problems at school.

Risks that affect your health are more complicated when they are cumulative risks (KYOO•myuh•luh•tiv), which occur *when one risk factor adds to another to increase danger.* For example, making unhealthy food choices is one risk. Not getting regular physical activity is another risk. Add these two risks together over time, and you raise your risk of developing diseases such as heart disease and cancer.

Many choices you make affect your health. Knowing the consequences of your choices and behaviors can help you take responsibility for your health.

Reducing Risks

Practicing prevention, *taking steps to avoid something,* is the best way to deal with risks. For example, wear a helmet when you ride a bike to help prevent head injury. Slow down when walking or running on wet or icy pavement to help prevent a fall. Prevention also means watching out for possible dangers. When you know dangers are ahead, you can avoid them and prevent accidents.

Physical injury can be a consequence of risk behaviors.

ERproductions Ltd/Blend Images LLC

STAYING INFORMED You can take responsibility for your health by staying informed. Learn about developments in health to maintain your own health. Getting a physical exam at least once a year by a doctor is another way to stay informed about your health.

CHOOSING ABSTINENCE
If you practice abstinence from risk behaviors, you care for your own health and others' health by preventing illness and injury. Abstinence is *the conscious, active choice not to participate in high-risk behaviors.* By choosing not to use tobacco, you may avoid getting lung cancer. By staying away from alcohol, illegal drugs, and sexual activity, you avoid the negative consequences of these risk behaviors.

Abstinence is good for all sides of your health triangle. It promotes your physical health by helping you avoid injury and illness. It protects your mental/emotional health by giving you peace of mind. It also benefits your relationships with family members, peers, and friends. Practicing abstinence shows you are taking responsibility for your personal health behaviors and that you respect yourself and others. You can feel good about making positive health choices, which will strengthen your mental/emotional health as well as your social health.

✓ Plan ahead.

✓ Think about consequences.

✓ Resist negative pressure from others.

✓ Stay away from risk takers.

✓ Pay attention to what you are doing.

✓ Know your limits.

✓ Be aware of dangers.

Reducing risk behaviors will help maintain your overall health.

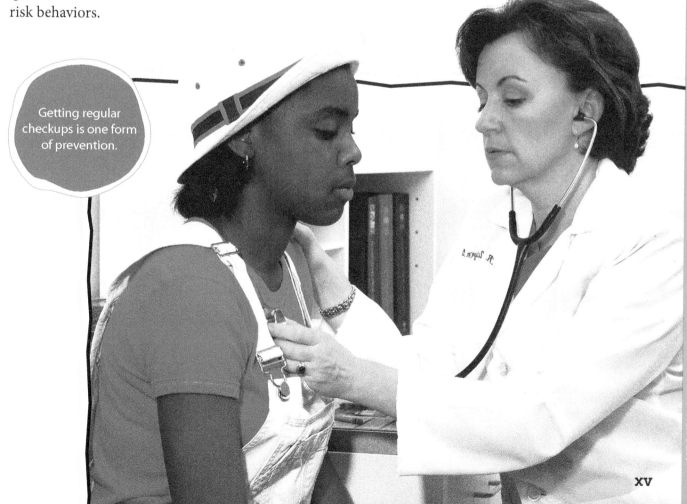

Getting regular checkups is one form of prevention.

Building Health Skills

SKILLS FOR A HEALTHY LIFE

Health skills are *skills that help you become and stay healthy.* Health skills can help you improve your physical, mental/emotional, and social health. Just as you learn math, reading, sports, and other kinds of skills, you can learn skills for taking care of your health now and for your entire life.

> These ten skills affect your physical, mental/emotional, and social health and can benefit you throughout your life.

Health Skills	What It Means to You
Accessing Information	You know how to find valid and reliable health information and health-promoting products and services.
Practicing Healthful Behaviors	You take action to reduce risks and protect yourself against illness and injury.
Stress Management	You find healthy ways to reduce and manage stress in your life.
Analyzing Influences	You recognize the many factors that influence your health, including culture, media, and technology.
Communication Skills	You express your ideas and feelings and listen when others express theirs.
Refusal Skills	You can say no to risky behaviors.
Conflict-Resolution Skills	You can work out problems with others in healthful ways.
Decision Making	You think through problems and find healthy solutions.
Goal Setting	You plan for the future and work to make your plans come true.
Advocacy	You take a stand for the common good and make a difference in your home, school, and community.

SELF-MANAGEMENT SKILLS

When you were younger, your parents and other adults decided what was best for your health. Now that you are older, you make many of these decisions for yourself. You take care of your personal health. You are developing your self-management skills. Two key self-management skills are practicing healthful behaviors and managing stress. When you eat healthy foods and get enough sleep, you are taking actions that promote good health. Stress management is learning to cope with challenges that put a strain on you mentally or emotionally.

Practicing Healthful Behaviors

Your behaviors affect your physical, mental/emotional, and social health. You will see benefits quickly when you practice healthful behaviors. If you exercise regularly, your heart and muscles grow stronger. When you eat healthful foods and drink plenty of water, your body works well.

Getting a good night's sleep will help you wake up with more energy. Respecting and caring for others will help you develop healthy relationships. Managing your feelings in positive ways will help you avoid actions you may regret later.

Staying **positive** is a **good health** habit.

Practicing healthful behaviors can help prevent injury, illness, and other health problems. When you practice healthful actions, you can help your total health. Your total health means your physical, mental/emotional, and social health. This means you take care of yourself and do not take risks. It means you learn health-promoting habits. When you eat well-balanced meals and

healthful snacks and get regular physical checkups you are practicing good health habits. Staying positive is another good health habit.

Managing Stress

Learning ways to deal with stress, *the body's response to real or imagined dangers or other life events,* is an important self-management skill. Stress management can help you learn ways to deal with stress. Stress management means identifying sources of stress. It also means you learn how to handle stress in ways that support good health. Relaxation is a good way to deal with stress. Exercise is another way to positively deal with stress.

Studying for a test can cause stress.

Making Decisions *and* Setting Goals

The path to good health begins with making good decisions. You may make more of your own decisions now. Some of those decisions might be deciding which clothes to buy or which classes to take.

As you grow older, you gain more freedom, but with it comes more responsibility. You will need to understand the short-term and long-term consequences of decisions.

Another responsibility is goal setting. You also need to plan how to reach those goals.

When you learn how to set realistic goals, you take a step toward health and well-being. Learning to make decisions and to set goals will help give you purpose and direction in your life.

ACCESSING INFORMATION

Knowing how to get reliable, or *trust-wor-thy and dependable,* health information is an important skill. Where can you find all this information? A main source is from adults you can trust. Community resources give you other ways to get information. These include the library and government health agencies. Organizations such as the American Red Cross can also provide good information.

Reliable Sources

You can find facts about health and health-enhancing products or services through media sources such as television, radio, and the Internet. TV and radio interviews with health professionals can give you information about current scientific studies related to health.

Web sites that end in .gov and .edu are often the most reliable sites. These sites are maintained by government organizations and educational institutions.

Getting health information is important, but so is analyzing whether that health information is valid, or reliable. Carefully review web sites ending in .org.

Many of these sites are maintained by organizations, such as the American Cancer Society or American Diabetes Association. However, some sites ending in .org may not be legitimate.

The Internet can be a good source of health information.

SW Productions/Getty Images

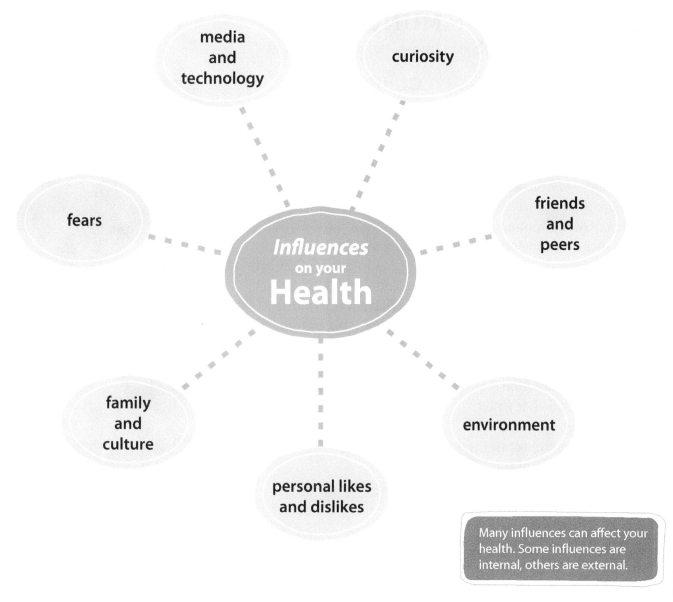

media
and
technology

curiosity

fears

Influences
on your
Health

friends
and
peers

family
and
culture

environment

personal likes
and dislikes

Many influences can affect your health. Some influences are internal, others are external.

Analyzing Influences

Learning how to analyze health information, products, and services will help you act in ways that protect your health. The first step in analyzing an influence is to identify its source. A TV commercial may tell you a certain food has health benefits.

Your **decisions** have to do with your *own* **values** and **beliefs.**

Ask yourself who is the source of the information. Next, think about the motive, or reason, for the influence. Does the advertiser really take your well-being into consideration? Does the ad make you curious about the product?

Does it try to scare you into buying the product? Analyzing influences involves recognizing factors that affect or influence your health.

Your decisions also have to do with your own values and beliefs. The opinions of your friends and family members affect your decisions. Your culture and messages from the media also affect your decisions.

SKILLS FOR COMMUNICATING WITH OTHERS

Your relationships with others depend on maintaining good communication skills. Communication is *the exchange of information through the use of words or actions.* Good communication skills include telling others how you feel. They also include listening to others and understanding how others feel. Two types of communication exist. They are verbal and nonverbal communication. Verbal communication involves a speaker or writer, and a listener or reader. Nonverbal communication includes tone of voice, body position, and using expressions.

Refusal Skills

An important communication skill is saying no. It may be something that is wrong. It may be something that you are not comfortable doing. You may worry what will happen if you don't go along with the group. Will your friends still like you? Will you still be a part of the group? It is at these times that refusal skills, or *strategies that help you say no effectively,* can help. Using refusal skills can sometimes be challenging, but they can help you stay true to yourself and to your beliefs. Also, other people will have respect for you for being honest.

Conflict Resolution

Conflicts, or disagreements with others, are part of life. Learning to deal with them in a healthy way is important. Conflict resolution is *a life skill that involves solving a disagreement in a way that satisfies both sides.* Conflict-resolution skills can help you find a way to satisfy everyone. Also, by using this positive health behavior, you can keep conflicts from getting out of hand.

Conflict resolution skills can help you find a way to satisfy everyone.

Advocacy

People with advocacy skills *take action in support of a cause.* They work to bring about a change by speaking out for something like health and wellness. When you speak out for health, you encourage other people to live healthy lives. Advocacy also means keeping others informed.

Using refusal skills effectively can help you avoid potentially dangerous situation.

Image Source/Getty Images

Making Decisions *and* Setting Goals

DECISIONS AND YOUR HEALTH

As you grow up, you usually gain more privileges. Along with privileges comes responsibility. You will make more of your own decisions. The choices and decisions you make can affect each part of your health triangle.

As you get older, you will learn to make more important decisions. You will need to understand the short-term and long-term consequences of the decisions you make.

You can learn the skill of making good decisions.

Some decisions may help you avoid harmful behaviors. These questions can help you understand some of the consequences of health-related decisions.

- How will this decision affect my health?
- Will it affect the health of others? If so, how?
- Is the behavior I might choose harmful or illegal?
- How will my family feel about my decision?
- Does this decision fit with my values?
- How will this decision affect my goals?

THE DECISION-MAKING PROCESS

You make decisions every day. Some decisions are easy to make. Other decisions are more difficult. Understanding the process of **decision making,** or *the process of making a choice or solving a problem,* will help you make the best possible decisions. The decision-making process can be broken down into six steps. You can apply these six steps to any decision you need to make.

Step 1: State the Situation

Identify the situation as you understand it. When you understand the situation and your choices you can make a sound decision. Ask yourself: What choice do you need to make? What are the facts? Who else is involved?

Step 2: List the Options

When you feel like you understand your situation, think of your options. List all of the possibilities you can think of. Be sure to include only those options that are safe. It is also important to ask an adult you trust for advice when making an important decision.

Step 3: Weigh the Possible Outcomes

After listing your options, you need to evaluate the consequences of each option. The word H.E.L.P. can be used to work through this step of the decision-making process.

- **H** (Healthful) What health risks will this option present to me and to others?
- **E** (Ethical) Does this choice reflect what my family and I believe to be ethical, or right? Does this choice show respect for me and others?
- **L** (Legal) Will I be breaking the law? Is this legal for someone my age?
- **P** (Parent Approval) Would my parents approve of this choice?

Step 4: Consider Your Values

Always consider your values or the beliefs that guide the way you live. Your values reflect what is important to you and what you have learned is right and wrong. Honesty, respect, consideration, and good health are values.

Step 5: Make a Decision and Act

You've weighed your options. You've considered the risks and consequences. Now you're ready for action. Choose the option that seems best for you. Remember that this step is not complete until you take action.

Step 6: Evaluate the Decision

Evaluating the results can help you make better decisions in the future. To evaluate the results, ask yourself: Was the outcome positive or negative? Were there any unexpected outcomes? Was there anything you could have done differently? How did your decision affect others? Do you think you made the right decision? What have you learned from the experience? If the outcome was not what you expected, try again.

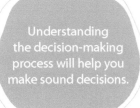

Understanding the decision-making process will help you make sound decisions.

Step 1
State the situation.

Step 2
List the options.

Step 3
Weigh the possible outcomes.

Step 4
Consider your values.

Step 5
Make a decision and act.

Step 6
Evaluate the decision.

SETTING REALISTIC GOALS

When you think about your future, what do you see? Do you see someone who has graduated from college and has a good job? Are there things you want to achieve? Answering these questions can give you an idea of your goals in life. A goal is something you want to accomplish.

Goal setting is *the process of working toward something you want to accomplish.* When you have learned to set realistic goals, they can help you focus on what you want to accomplish in life. Realistic goals are goals you can reach.

Setting goals can benefit your health. Many goals can help to improve your overall health. Think about all you want to accomplish in life. Do you need to set some health-related goals to be able to accomplish those things?

Goals can become milestones and can tell you how far you have come. Reaching goals can be a powerful boost to your self-confidence. Improving your self-confidence can help to strengthen your mental/emotional health.

Types of Goals

There are two basic types of goals—short-term goals, *goals that you can achieve in a short length of time,* and long-term goals, *goals that you plan to reach over an extended period of time.* As the names imply, short-term goals can be accomplished more quickly than long-term goals.

Reaching goals can be a **powerful** boost to your self confidence.

Getting your homework turned in on time might be a short-term goal. Long-term goals are generally accomplished over months or years. Getting a college education might be a long-term goal. Often long-term goals are made up of short-term goals.

Reaching Your Goals

To accomplish your short-term and long-term goals, you need a plan. A goal-setting plan that has a series of steps for you to take can be very effective in helping you accomplish your goals. Following a plan can help you make the best use of your time, energy, and other resources. Here are the steps of a goal-setting plan:

- Step 1: Identify a specific goal and write it down. Write down exactly what your goal is. Be sure the goal is realistic.
- Step 2: List the steps to reach your goal. Breaking big goals into smaller goals can make them easier to accomplish.
- Step 3: Get help and support from others. There are many people in your life who can help you reach your goals. They may be parents, teachers, coaches, or other trusted adults.
- Step 4: Evaluate your progress. Check periodically to see if you are actually progressing toward your goal. You may have to identify and consider how to overcome an obstacle before moving toward your goal.
- Step 5: Celebrate when you reach your goal. Give yourself a reward.

©moodboard/Corbis

Jamie has set a goal to be chosen for the all-star team

Choosing Health Services

WHAT IS HEALTH CARE?

You will probably at some point need to seek health care services. Health care provides services that promote, maintain, or restore health to individuals or communities. The health care system is all the medical care available to a nation's people, the way they receive the care, and the way the care is paid for. It is through the health care system that people receive medical services.

← Emergency

HEALTH CARE PROVIDERS

Many different professionals can help you with your health care. You may be most familiar with your own doctor who is your primary care provider: a health care professional who provides checkups and general care. Nurse practitioners and physician's assistants can also provide primary care.

In addition to doctors, nurse practitioners, and physician's assistants, many other health care professionals provide care. Nurses, pharmacists, health educators, counselors, mental health specialists, dentists, and nutritionists are all health care providers.

Preventive Care

Getting regular checkups is one way to prevent health problems and maintain wellness. During a checkup, your health care provider will check you carefully. She or he will check your heart and lungs and vision and hearing. You may also receive any immunizations you need. During your visit, your doctor may talk to you about healthful eating, exercise, avoiding alcohol, tobacco, and drugs, and other types of preventive care, or steps taken to keep disease or injury from happening or getting worse.

Specialists

Sometimes your primary care provider is not able to help you. In that case, he or she will refer you to a specialist, or health care professional trained to treat a special category of patients or specific health problems. Some specialists treat specific types of people. Other specialists treat specific conditions or body systems.

Different specialists treat different conditions.

Specialist	Specialty
Allergist	Asthma, hay fever, other allergies
Cardiologist	Heart problems
Dermatologist	Skin conditions and diseases
Oncologist	Cancer
Ophthalmologist	Eye diseases
Orthodontist	Tooth and jaw irregularities
Orthopedist	Broken bones and similar problems
Otolaryngologist	Ear, nose, and throat
Pediatrician	Infants, children, and teens

HEALTH CARE SETTINGS

Years ago, people were very limited as to where they could go for health care. In more recent years, new types of health care delivery settings have been developed. People now can go to their doctors' offices, hospitals, surgery centers, hospices, and assisted living communities.

Doctors' Offices

Doctors' offices are probably the most common setting for receiving health care. Your doctor, nurse practitioner, or physician's assistant has medical equipment to help them diagnose illnesses and to give checkups. Most of your medical needs can be met at your doctor's office.

Hospitals

If your medical needs cannot be met at your doctor's office, you may need to go to the hospital. Hospitals have much more medical equipment for diagnosing and treating illnesses. They have rooms for doing surgery and for emergency medicine. They have rooms for patients to stay overnight, if necessary. Hospitals have staff on duty around the clock every day of the year.

Surgery Centers

Your doctor may recommend that you go to a surgery center rather than a hospital. Surgery centers are facilities that offer outpatient surgical care. This means that the patients do not stay overnight. They go home the same day they have the surgery. Serious surgeries cannot be done in a surgery center. They would be done in a hospital where the patient can stay and recover. For general outpatient care, many people go to clinics.

Clinics

Clinics are similar to doctors' offices and often have primary care physicians and specialists on staff. If you go to a clinic, you might not see the same doctor each time you go. You might see whoever is on duty that day. This might make it more difficult for the doctor to get to know you and your health issues. However, for people who do not need to go to the doctor often, a clinic might be a good fit.

Hospice Care

Hospice care provides a place where terminally ill patients can live out the remainder of their lives. Terminally ill patients will not recover from their illness. Hospice workers are specially trained and are experts in pain management. They are also trained and skilled at giving emotional support to the family and the patient. Many terminally ill patients receive hospice care in their own homes. Nurses visit the patient in their own home and provide medications for pain. They also spend time with family members, helping them learn to cope during the emotionally difficult time.

Pixtal/AGE Fotostock

Assisted Living Communities

As people get older, they may not be able to take care of themselves as well as they used to. Assisted living communities offer older people an alternative to nursing homes. In nursing homes, all of the resident's needs are taken care of. In assisted living communities, the residents can choose which services they need. They may be unable to drive and need transportation. They may need reminders to take medications. They may need to have food prepared for them. In an assisted living community, the residents are able to live in their own apartments as long as they are able. Medical staff is available when the residents need help.

PAYING FOR HEALTH CARE

Health care costs can be expensive. Many people buy health insurance to help pay for medical costs. Health insurance is a plan in which a person pays a set fee to an insurance company in return for the company's agreement to pay some or all medical expenses when needed. They pay a monthly premium, or fee, to the health insurance company for the policy. There are several different options when choosing health insurance.

Private Health Care Plans

One health insurance option is managed care. Health insurance plans emphasize preventative medicine and work to control the cost and maintain the quality of health care. Using managed care, patients save money when they visit doctors who participate in the managed care plan. There are several different managed care plans such as a health maintenance organization (HMO), a preferred provider organization (PPO), and a point-of-service (POS) plan.

Government Public Health Care Plans

The government currently offers two types of health insurance—Medicaid and Medicare. Medicaid is for people with limited income. Medicare is for people over the age of 65 and for people of any age with certain disabilities.

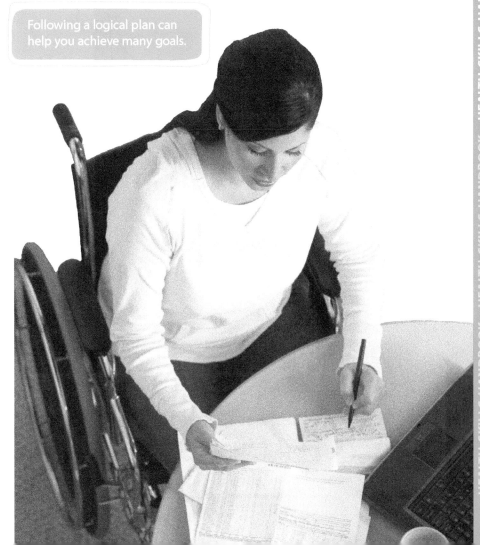

Following a logical plan can help you achieve many goals.

Safety

PREMIUM ONLINE RESOURCES

 Audio

 Videos

 Bilingual Glossary

 Fitness Zone

 Web Quest

 Review

Performing activities safely lowers the risk of accidents. *Describe two ways you can avoid accidents.*

Building Safe Habits

BIG IDEA Being safety conscious means being aware that safety is important and acting safely.

Before You Read

QUICK WRITE List three examples of accidental injuries that people experience. After reading the lesson, check to see whether you were correct.

 Video

As You Read

FOLDABLES Study Organizer

Make the Foldable® on page 54 to record the information presented in Lesson 1.

Vocabulary

› accident
› accidental injuries
› safety conscious
› hazard
› accident chain

 Audio

 Bilingual Glossary

Developing Good Character

Responsibility When you put your belongings in their proper place, they are not in the way, so they're less likely to cause accidents. Putting away clothes and equipment also helps cut down on clutter. *Describe what else you can do to help prevent accidents.*

SAFETY FIRST

MAIN IDEA Accidents and accidental injuries can affect people of all ages.

You've probably heard warnings such as, "Buckle up!" and "Look both ways before you cross the street," for as long as you can remember. You might have helped teach these safe habits to a younger brother or sister. An **accident** is *any event that was not intended to happen.* Accidents do happen, but you can prevent many of them. When you stay safe and avoid accidents, you help yourself and those around you stay healthy.

You might not think serious accidents can happen to you. However, the Centers for Disease Control and Prevention (CDC) reports that accidental injuries are the leading cause of death in teens. **Accidental injuries** are *injuries resulting from an accident.* Accidental injuries are the fifth leading cause of death in the United States across all age groups.

When you *stay safe* and *avoid accidents,* you **help yourself** and those around you *stay healthy.*

The leading causes of nonfatal accidental injuries include falls, being struck or cut by something, being bitten or stung, overexertion, and poisoning.

The first step in staying safe is being safety conscious. To be **safety-conscious** means *being aware that safety is important and careful to act in a safe manner.* It is easier to prevent injuries than to treat them. Think ahead. Know how to spot a **hazard** or *potential source of danger.*

Reading Check

EXPLAIN *What is the difference between an accident and an accidental injury?*

Fuse/Getty Images

HOW ACCIDENTS HAPPEN

MAIN IDEA For any accident to occur, three elements must be present.

Accidents happen when people stop being safety conscious. Think back to your last accident and the accident chain that led up to it. An accident chain is *a series of events that include a situation, an unsafe habit, and an unsafe action.* For any accident to occur, these three elements must be present.

Breaking *the* Accident Chain

Look at the links in Tony's accident chain below. Breaking just one link would have kept Tony from being injured.

> Many accidents can be avoided. *How could Tony avoid this accident?*

- **Change the Situation.** Tony could have gotten up earlier. He could have set his alarm for a reasonable time. He could have asked a family member to wake him if he overslept.
- **Change the Unsafe Habit.** Tony may have avoided the accident by storing his books on a bookshelf or placing them in his book bag.
- **Change the Unsafe Action.** Tony could have paid attention to where he was going. He could have slowed down and watched his step.

Being safety conscious might have kept Tony from tripping and falling. By changing the situation, the unsafe habit, or the unsafe action, Tony could have prevented his accident.

REVIEW

 After You Read

1. **VOCABULARY** Define *accident.* Use the word in an original sentence.
2. **IDENTIFY** What are the five links in the accident chain?
3. **GIVE EXAMPLES** What are three ways to break the accident chain?

>>> **Thinking Critically**

4. **APPLY** Benny has always had a bookshelf on the wall next to his bed. Now that he is taller, the bookshelf has become a problem. In fact, this year Benny has bumped his head on the shelf three times. What should he do to be safer?
5. **ANALYZE** Grant's friend dared him to walk across a narrow 12-foot-high fence. What should Grant do, and why?

>>> **Applying Health Skills**

6. **DECISION MAKING** Tina wants to go bike riding with a friend, but she left her helmet in her dad's truck. What are Tina's options? Use decision making skills to help Tina make a safe decision.

⟳ Review

🔊 Audio

1. **The Situation** Tony has overslept. He wakes up in a panic. The bus is coming in 15 minutes.

3. **The Unsafe Action** Without looking where he is going, Tony runs to the bathroom to wash up.

5. **The Result** When Tony falls, he sprains his wrist. He misses his bus and is in a lot of pain.

2. **The Unsafe Habit** Tony didn't put his books away from the night before. He just left them on the floor.

4. **The Accident** Tony trips over his books and falls down.

Safety *at* Home *and* School

BIG IDEA Following safety rules can keep you safe both at home and away from home.

Before You Read

QUICK WRITE What is the first thing that you should do if you think the building you are in is on fire? Write a sentence or two describing the action you would take.

 Video

As You Read

STUDY ORGANIZER Make the study organizer on page 54 to record the information presented in Lesson 2.

Vocabulary

> flammable
> electrical overload
> smoke alarm
> fire extinguisher

 Audio

 Bilingual Glossary

Myth vs. Fact

Myth: Small fires are not a major concern and can be controlled.
Fact: A fire of any size needs immediate attention. Small fires can become uncontrollable fires very quickly. A fire that starts with material burning in a wastebasket in the room can spread to two rooms within four minutes. Smoke alarms and sprinkler systems play an important role in fire safety. In homes with smoke alarms, the risk of dying in a fire is reduced by 50 percent compared to homes without working smoke alarms. In homes with both smoke alarms and a sprinkler system, the risk of death is reduced by 82 percent.

SAFETY IN THE HOME

MAIN IDEA Your home may be filled with many potential safety hazards, such as stairs or appliances.

Jessica and her family are moving into a new home. As Jessica looks around her new room on the second floor, her father says, "We'll need to store an emergency ladder in your room." He then added, "This window is your emergency exit in case of fire."

Home is a place where everyone should feel safe and comfortable. Yet, homes can contain hazards. Stairways or spilled water can lead to falls, the most common type of home injury. Appliances can cause electrical shocks.

> *Home is a place where everyone should feel safe and comfortable.*

Sharp tools in the kitchen or garage, such as knives, saws, and screwdrivers can lead to cuts. Other injuries can result from poisonings, choking, drowning, and guns. Fires are the third leading cause of unintentional injury and death in the home. Overall, about 45 percent of deaths from accidental injuries occur in and around the home.

However, injuries from these hazards can be avoided. Following safety rules can reduce the risks of home hazards.

>> Reading Check

EXPLAIN *Why is it important to follow safety rules at home?*

Preventing Falls

Most falls in the home occur in the kitchen, the bathroom, or on the stairs. These safety rules can help you prevent falls.

KITCHEN SAFETY Clean up spills right away. Use a stepstool, not a chair, to get items that are out of reach. Avoid running on wet or waxed floors.

BATHROOM SAFETY Put a nonskid mat near the tub or shower. Use rugs that have a rubber backing to prevent the rug from slipping. Keep personal products in plastic bottles.

STAIRCASE SAFETY Keep staircases well lit and clear of all objects. Apply nonslip treads to slippery stairs. Make sure handrails are secure and stable. If small children live in the house, put gates at the top and bottom of the stairs.

Preventing Poisonings

Many common household products are poisonous. Items such as cleaning products, insecticides, medications, and vitamins can be harmful if not used or taken as directed. Accidental poisoning can occur by swallowing, absorbing through the skin, injection from a needle, or breathing poisonous fumes.

To help keep the people in your home safe from poisoning, make sure that labels on containers of household products are clearly marked. Store cleaning products, insecticides, and other potential poisons out of the reach of young children.

Never refer to a child's medicine or vitamins as candy. Be sure that all medicines are in bottles with childproof caps. Always use a product or medication as directed by the label.

Picking up toys that are left on steps can help prevent falls. *Describe other ways you can help prevent accidents in the home.*

Make sure that *labels* on containers of household products are **clearly marked.**

Gun Safety

In many states it is illegal for most teens to own a gun. If you find a gun, do not touch it. Call a parent, guardian, or other trusted adult immediately. If someone at school is carrying a gun or other weapon, tell an adult or school official.

The best way to prevent a gun accident in the home is to not have guns in the home. If a gun must be kept in the home, use the following safety precautions:

- Guns should have trigger locks and be stored unloaded in a locked cabinet.
- Ammunition should be stored in a separate locked cabinet.
  - Any person who handles a gun should be trained in gun safety.
    - All guns should be handled as if they are loaded.
    - *Never* play with a gun or point it at someone.

Electrical Safety

Improper use of electrical appliances or outlets can cause dangerous electrical shocks. To prevent electrical shocks, never use an electrical appliance around water or if you are wet. Unplug small appliances such as hair dryers when they are not in use. To unplug electrical appliances, gently pull the plug, not the cord. If a cord becomes frayed, don't use the appliance until it is repaired. Unplug any appliance that is not working properly. Avoid running cords under rugs. In homes with small children, cover unused outlets with plastic outlet protectors.

> **Reading Check**
>
> **LIST** *What are two ways to prevent electrical shocks?*

FIRE SAFETY

MAIN IDEA It is a healthy practice to have a fire safety plan, fire extinguisher, and working smoke alarms.

Fires happen in about 370,000 homes in the United States each year, killing approximately 2,800 people. The kitchen is where most fires start. A fire needs three elements to start—fuel, heat, and air. Sources of heat include cigarettes, matches, or electrical wires. If a heat source comes into contact with anything **flammable**, *substances that catch fire easily*, a fire can result. Household chemicals, rags, wood, or newspapers and magazines are all examples of flammable materials.

Other fires start from **electrical overload**, *a dangerous situation in which too much electric current flows along a single circuit*. Here are some safety guidelines to help you prevent home fires:

- Keep stoves and ovens clean. This will prevent food or grease from catching fire.
- Keep objects that can catch fire easily at least three feet away from portable heaters.
- Remind adults who smoke that they should never smoke in bed or on overstuffed furniture. Remind smokers to never toss a lit cigarette into the trash.
- Regularly inspect electrical wires, outlets, and appliances to make sure they are in proper working order. Never pull on the cord to unplug an appliance. Never run cords under rugs or carpets. If you notice worn or shredded cords, stop using the cord and tell an adult about it.

Fires happen in about **370,000 homes** in the United States each year.

- Discard old newspapers, oily rags, and other materials that burn easily.
- Use and store matches and lighters properly. Keep them out of the reach of young children. Don't leave candles burning unattended.

Careless cooking
Spattered grease and oil can cause kitchen fires. Unattended cooking pots can spill onto burners or in the oven.

Careless smoking
Cigarettes can start fires if people leave them unattended or fall asleep while they are still burning. Cigarettes can also start fires if people toss them into the trash when they are still burning.

Incorrect storage of flammable materials
Examples of flammable materials are paint, chemicals, oil, rags, and newspapers.

Damaged electrical systems or electrical overload
Fires can start due to too much current flowing through overloaded circuits. Shredded wires or torn cords can also lead to fires. Broken appliances can cause fires as well.

Gas leaks
Gas lines can leak and catch fire. Natural gas is odorless and colorless, so it has an additive that makes it smell. If you smell gas, first get out of the house, then call 911.

> **》 Reading Check**
>
> **RECALL** *What are three safety guidelines to help prevent fires?*

Almost all people killed in fires are children and older adults. *Explain why children and older adults are the most likely to die in house fires.*

Being Prepared in Case of Fire

The earlier you receive warning of a fire, the better your chances of getting out safely. Every level of a house should have smoke alarms. A **smoke alarm** is *a device that sounds an alarm when it senses smoke.* Smoke alarms are especially useful when you are sleeping. Install them as close to bedrooms as possible. Test smoke alarms every month. Replace batteries once a year.

Water will put out fires in which paper, wood, or cloth is burning. However, you should never use water to put out a fire that involves grease, oil, or electricity. That will actually make the fire worse. Instead, use a **fire extinguisher,** *a device that sprays chemicals that put out fires.* Every home should have a fire extinguisher. Read the directions, and make sure that you know how to use it properly.

Create a fire escape plan with your family. Choose a meeting point outside where everyone can gather in the event of a fire. Practice the escape plan with your family every six months.

If you are in a fire, you need to know what to do to escape safely. *Explain why you should get out first and then call 911.*

1. If possible, leave quickly. Get out of the building before calling 911 or the fire department.

2. Before opening a closed door, feel it to see if it is hot. If it is hot, do not open it. There may be flames just outside the door.

3. If you must exit through smoke, crawl along the floor. Smoke and hot air rise, so it is important to stay as low as possible. The air you breathe will be cleaner. The smoke will not be as likely to overcome you.

4. If you can't get out, stay in the room with the door closed. Roll up a blanket or towel and push it across the bottom of the door to keep out smoke. If there are phones in the room, call 911 or the fire department. Signal for help at the window with a light.

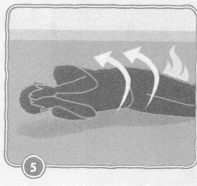

5. If your clothing catches fire, stop, drop, and roll. Rolling on the ground will smother the flames. Never run; the rush of air will fan the flames.

6. Once outside, go to the prearranged meeting point. Let everyone know that you are safe. Then someone should call 911 or the fire department. Never go back into a burning building.

SAFETY AT SCHOOL

MAIN IDEA Following rules at school helps you, other students, and teachers stay safe.

REVIEW

Your school probably has rules in place to keep students and teachers safe. Many accidental injuries at school can be avoided. Safety rules that protect the health and safety of students and teachers, may suggest that you:

Play by the rules. Rules are made to protect you and others. The cafeteria, classrooms, halls, gym, and auditorium may all have a separate set of important safety rules to follow.

Report weapons or unsafe activities. It's essential to follow rules prohibiting weapon possession at school. If you think that someone has brought a gun or other weapon to school, report the person immediately to a teacher or principal.

Wear necessary safety gear. Working in a science lab or playing sports are two places where appropriate gear will help keep you safe.

>> Reading Check

RECALL *What strategies can you and your peers use to stay safe at school?* ■

>>> After You Read

1. **VOCABULARY** Define the terms *smoke alarm* and *fire extinguisher*.
2. **IDENTIFY** List three strategies for preventing poisoning.
3. **DESCRIBE** How can you be prepared for a fire that might happen in your home?

>>> Thinking Critically

4. **APPLY** In what ways is a cluttered room a hazard?
5. **ANALYZE** Why is it a bad idea to call medicine "candy" to get children to take it?

>>> Applying Health Skills

6. **REFUSAL SKILLS** Will wants to see the hunting rifle that Troy's dad just bought. The rifle is in a locked case, but Troy knows where the key is. How could Troy refuse Will's request?

🔄 Review

🔊 Audio

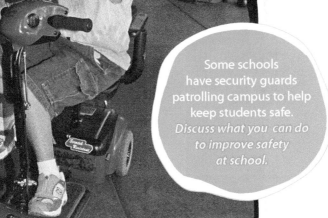

Some schools have security guards patrolling campus to help keep students safe. *Discuss what you can do to improve safety at school.*

Realistic Reflections

Safety *on the* Road *and* Outdoors

BIG IDEA Following safety rules can help prevent injury on the road and outdoors.

Before You Read

QUICK WRITE Write down three actions you take to stay safe when participating in outdoor activities.

▶ Video

As You Read

STUDY ORGANIZER Make the study organizer on page 54 to record the information presented in Lesson 3.

Vocabulary

› pedestrian
› defensive driving
› hypothermia

🔊 Audio

🔤 Bilingual Glossary

🏃 Fitness Zone

Increasing My Fitness for Hiking To increase my fitness level for hiking, I can fill my backpack with items I would take hiking and camping, put on my hiking boots or shoes, and walk for one hour several times a week. I can go to the park or walk in my neighborhood. This will help me get used to walking with some weight in my backpack and break in my shoes, while increasing my fitness level.

STAYING SAFE ON THE ROAD

MAIN IDEA Safety in vehicles includes wearing a safety belt and not distracting the driver.

In the United States, motor vehicle crashes are the leading cause of accidental deaths in people 1 to 24 years old. To be a safety-conscious passenger, wear a safety belt whenever you ride in a vehicle. Safety belts help keep you in your seat if your vehicle gets into a crash. Do not distract the driver of the vehicle. As many as 3,000 people per year are killed in accidents involving a distracted driver. Another way to stay safe is to never get in a car with a driver who has been drinking alcohol or using drugs. Call a trusted adult to pick you up instead.

Many cars have air bags, too. Air bags can help keep people in the front seats from colliding with the steering wheel and dashboard. However, the force of air bags can hurt small children.

The safest place for children to ride is in the back seat. Infants and small children should ride in an appropriate car seat or booster seat until they are large enough to use a safety belt.

Motor vehicle crashes are the **leading cause** of accidental deaths.

If you take the bus to school, don't bother the bus driver while he or she is driving. Don't get up while the bus is moving or put your arms out the window. When you get off the bus, make sure the bus driver and all drivers of the vehicles around the bus can see you clearly. Don't cross the street behind the bus. If you are in a bus during an emergency, cooperate with the driver so that you and everyone else on the bus remain safe.

Safety *on* Foot

Ever since you learned to walk, you have been a pedestrian, *a person who travels on foot.* Safety is important for pedestrians. Pay attention to what is happening around you. Follow these rules to become a safer pedestrian.

- Walk on the sidewalk if there is one. If there is no sidewalk, walk facing oncoming traffic, staying to the left side of the road.
- Cross streets only at crosswalks. Do not cross the street in the middle of the block.
- Look both ways several times before crossing, and keep looking and listening for oncoming cars.
- If you cross in front of a stopped vehicle, be sure the driver can see you. Make eye contact with him or her before stepping in front of the vehicle.
- Obey all traffic signals.
- During the day, wear bright clothing. If you walk at night, take a well-lit route. Wear light-colored or reflective clothing and carry a flashlight.
- Do not talk on a cell phone or wear headphones as you walk. Always be aware of your surroundings.

Safety *on* Wheels

Riding bicycles and using skates, in-line skates, skateboards, and scooters are activities many teens enjoy. One way to prevent injury while participating in these activities is to learn about the risks and then follow rules to avoid them.

Always wear an appropriate helmet and other safety gear. Make sure your clothing fits well and does not prohibit you from moving freely.

Bicycle riders need to obey the same traffic rules as drivers. *Describe what else bicycle riders should do to stay safe.*

Head injuries cause 70 to 80 percent of the deaths from bicycle accidents. Wearing a helmet every time you get on your bike can reduce your risk of head injury by 85 percent. It is also important for bicycle riders to ride with the flow of traffic and obey traffic signs and signals. Bicyclists should never weave through traffic. When riding with a friend, ride in single file, not side-by-side. Learn hand signals, and use them before turning or changing lanes.

Both bicyclists and drivers must practice defensive driving, which means *watching out for other people on the road and anticipating unsafe acts.*

Bicyclists should be visible to others by wearing bright, reflective clothes. Bicycles should have lights and reflectors. To reduce risk of injury while bicycling, do not ride at night or in bad weather.

Skates, in-line skates, skateboards, and scooters can be a fun, but only when they are used safely. Here are some guidelines for having fun while staying injury free.

- Wear protective gear, including a hard-shell helmet, wrist guards, gloves, elbow pads, and knee pads.
- Do not speed.
- Follow your community's rules on where you can ride your skateboard or scooter. Avoid skating or riding in parking lots, streets, and other areas with traffic.
- Practice a safe way to fall on a soft surface.
- Don't skate or ride a scooter after dark.
- Avoid riding or skating on wet, dirty, or uneven surfaces.

>> **Reading Check**

GIVE EXAMPLES *Name three ways to stay safe on wheels.*

STAYING SAFE OUTDOORS

Outdoor activities are more fun when you "play it safe." To stay safe while enjoying outdoor activities, remember to:

Use good judgment. Plan ahead. Check the weather forecast. Make sure you have the proper safety gear for each activity and that what you are doing is safe. If you are unsure, ask a trusted adult.

Take a buddy or two. Be sure you are with at least one other person. Always tell your parent or guardian where you are going.

Warm up and cool down. To prevent injuries, stretch after your warm-up and cool down.

Stay aware. Learn the signs of weather emergencies. When necessary, move quickly to shelter for safety.

Know your limits. Be aware of your skills and abilities. For example, if you are a beginning swimmer, don't try to swim a long distance.

Protect your skin. Wear bug protection and sunscreen. It is important to wear sunscreen to protect your skin from the sun's damaging rays.

Planning for Weather

When planning your activity, always check the weather. One major risk is an electrical storm. If you are outdoors during an electrical storm, try to find shelter in a building or car. Follow safety tips for hot weather and cold weather.

When planning your activity, always check the weather.

During hot weather, your body can overheat. If you feel dizzy, out of breath, or have a headache, take a break. Keep cool by drinking plenty of water. Rest in the shade when you can. Overworking your body in the heat can lead to two dangerous conditions: heat exhaustion and heatstroke. Signs of heat exhaustion can include cold, clammy skin, dizziness, or nausea.

Signs of heatstroke can include an increase in body temperature, difficulty breathing, and a loss of consciousness. Heatstroke can be deadly. If someone shows signs of heatstroke, call 911 and get medical help right away.

Cold weather can be dangerous if your body or parts of your body get too cold. When you are outside in cold weather, dress in layers. Wear a hat, warm footwear, and gloves or mittens. Anyone who starts to feel very cold or shiver should go inside and get warm. It is important to drink plenty of water and take a break when you feel tired. Also, wearing sunscreen is important in both warm and cold weather. While performing some winter activities, such as skiing, you are exposed to the sun. Wearing sunscreen and sunglasses will help to protect your skin from harmful UV rays.

Planning your trip can make it safer and more fun.

©Fancy/Veer

Health SKILLS ACTIVITY

Preventing *Drowning*

Use library and Internet resources to research drowning and how it can be prevented. Take notes on what you learn. With your teacher, invite a water safety instructor to visit your class. Have the instructor explain ways to avoid drowning in both warm and cold water.

On Your Own
Create a video or poster that shows and describes the different drowning prevention techniques for warm and cold water.

Water Safety

Water activities can be a lot of fun. To avoid injury, you should learn and follow water safety rules. Know how to swim well. Good swimmers are less likely to panic in an emergency.

Follow these other tips to stay safe in the water.
- Swim only when a lifeguard or other trusted adult is present.
- Swim with a buddy.
- Monitor yourself. Don't swim if you are tired or cold, or if you have been out in the sun for too long.

- Look around your environment often. Watch for signs of storms. If you are swimming when a storm begins, get out of the water right away.
- Avoid swimming in water with strong currents.
- Dive only in areas that are marked as safe for diving. The American Red Cross suggests that water be at least nine feet deep for diving or jumping. Avoid diving into unfamiliar water or into above-ground pools that may be shallow.
- If you are responsible for children, watch them closely. Avoid letting them near the water unless there is a trained lifeguard on duty. Accidents can happen even in small wading pools.
- When boating or waterskiing, wear a life jacket at all times. If the water is cold, wear a wetsuit. This will protect you from developing **hypothermia** (hy·poh·THER·mee·uh), *a sudden and dangerous drop in body temperature.*

Swimming in an area where a lifeguard is present is one way to stay safe while in the water. *Identify what else you can do to stay safe while in the water.*

Brand X Pictures/Getty Images

Safety on the Trail

Preparation is the first step in a safe and enjoyable hike or camping trip. Follow the tips listed below to help you stay safe while hiking and camping.

Never camp or hike alone. Make sure family members know your route and your expected date and time of return. Carry a cell phone or long-range walkie-talkie.

Dress properly. Be aware of the weather and dress accordingly. Dress in layers and wear long pants to protect yourself against ticks. If you are hiking up a mountain, know that the weather may change as you change altitude. Wear sturdy footwear. Before you hike in any shoes or boots, break them in to avoid getting blisters.

Bring equipment and supplies. You should have a map of the area in which you will be hiking or camping. Learn how to read a compass. Take along a first aid kit, flashlight, and extra batteries. Be sure to bring an adequate supply of drinking water and food for your trip. Bring food that will not spoil.

Know the plants and animals. Learn to recognize the dangerous plants and animals in your area so that you can avoid them. For example, learn what poison ivy and poison oak look like. To avoid insect bites and stings, tuck your pant legs into your socks and apply insect repellent. Learn first aid to treat reactions to poisonous plants, insects, and snakebites.

Use fire responsibly. Learn the proper way to build a campfire. Light campfires only where permitted. Put out all campfires completely before you go to sleep or leave the campsite. To put out a campfire, soak it with water or cover it completely with sand or dirt that is free of debris.

> **Reading Check**
>
> IDENTIFY *What safety items should you bring on a hike or camping trip?* ▪

Safe hiking and camping takes planning. *Explain why it is important to let people know where you are hiking and when you plan to return.*

REVIEW

After You Read

1. **DEFINE** What is a *pedestrian*?
2. **EXPLAIN** Why is it important to learn how to fall when skating or riding a bike?
3. **IDENTIFY** Name three ways to stay safe while in the water.

Thinking Critically

4. **ANALYZE** What are some safety factors that can reduce your risk of traffic injuries?
5. **EVALUATE** How does practicing the buddy system help keep you safe outdoors?

Applying Health Skills

6. **ADVOCACY** Create a poster that displays the dangerous plants in your area. Show plants such as poison ivy or poison oak as well as plants that are poisonous if eaten. Post a phone number to call if someone has eaten a poisonous plant.

🄲 Review
🔊 Audio

Anne Ackermann/Getty Images

Personal Safety *and* Online Safety

BIG IDEA You can protect yourself from violence by avoiding dangerous situations.

Before You Read

QUICK WRITE What steps do you take to keep yourself safe? Write a short paragraph about these strategies.

 Video

As You Read

STUDY ORGANIZER Make the study organizer on page 54 to record the information presented in Lesson 4.

Vocabulary

› precautions

 Audio

 Bilingual Glossary

Developing Good Character

Responsibility When you take steps to protect yourself when you are at home, on the street, or online, you are taking responsibility for your own safety. Taking responsibility for your personal safety is an important part of the health triangle. You can protect yourself from physical violence, you can feel confident about yourself, and you may feel less stress about situations that made you nervous before.

PERSONAL SAFETY

MAIN IDEA You can reduce your risk of becoming a victim of violence by avoiding unsafe situations.

Did you know that teens are the victims of violence more than any other age group? Violence is physical force used to harm people or damage property. Teens are more likely than children to go out at night and less likely to protect their personal safety than adults.

If a situation feels unsafe, it probably is.

Personal safety refers to the steps you take to prevent yourself from becoming the victim of a crime. You can reduce your risk of becoming a victim of violence by avoiding unsafe situations. Be alert to your surroundings, and trust your instincts. If a situation feels unsafe, it probably is unsafe.

Staying Safe at Home

Staying safe at home involves observing safety rules such as the ones listed below.

- When you're home, keep your doors and windows locked. Only open the door for someone you know, or not at all if your parents tell you not to answer the door.
- When you answer the phone or use the Internet, avoid offering personal information. Never tell a stranger that you are home alone. If the person asks to speak to your parents, say that parents are busy and are not able to come to the phone at this time.
- When you come home, have your key ready before you reach the door.
- If someone comes to the door or window and you feel you are in danger, call 911.

Reading Check

DESCRIBE *How can you reduce the risk of becoming a victim of violence?*

Onoky/Getty Images

Staying Safe on the Street

Before going out, tell your family where you are going and how you will get there. Make sure they also know when you expect to return. Don't walk by yourself, if possible. After dark, walk in well-lit areas. Stay in familiar neighborhoods; avoid deserted streets and shortcuts. If you think someone is following you, go into a public place.

Some public places that offer safety include a store or a well-lit area with other people nearby.

Try not to look like an easy target. Stand tall and walk confidently. Never carry your wallet, purse, or backpack in a way that is easy for others to grab. If someone wants your money or possessions, give them up.

Avoid strangers. Never get into or go near a stranger's car or hitchhike. Do not enter a building with a stranger. Don't agree to run errands or do other tasks for strangers. If someone tries to grab you, scream and run away. Go to the nearest place with people. Ask them to call 911 or your parents.

> **Reading Check**
>
> **EXPLAIN** *Why is it important to tell your family where you are going and when to expect you home?*

ONLINE SAFETY

MAIN IDEA Staying safe online is an important part of your overall safety.

Whether for schoolwork or fun, it's almost impossible to avoid using the Internet. However, you can avoid the dangers that might be lurking online by taking precautions, or *planned actions taken before an event to increase the chances of a safe outcome.* The Internet is like any tool. You've got to use it right to stay safe.

Protecting Your Data

Protecting your personal data helps keep people from stealing your usernames and passwords, which can lead to identity theft. Use the following tips to help protect your data while using the Internet.

Don't give out personal information. Some people may not be telling the truth about themselves. By not including personal information, you are taking the best action to avoid becoming the victim of a cyberbully as well.

The Internet is like any tool. You've got to use it right to stay safe.

Taking precautions when using the Internet helps protect your safety. *What are ways you can protect your personal data?*

Be wary of attachments or links in e-mails. Don't click on links that are sent in e-mails from strangers. If you open an attachment from a stranger, you might be inviting a virus into your computer. Run a virus scan before opening any attachments—even if you know the sender. He or she could be sending a virus without even knowing it.

Be careful about downloads. Download applications from reputable sites. Otherwise, the applications could come with viruses and spyware attached.

Keep passwords private. Never reveal them to people online.

Use filtering software. Search engines can filter information that's not meant for you. Use the "preferences" tab to set it up.

Get permission. Ask a trusted adult before heading online—and especially before filling out any forms on the Internet.

Avoiding Internet Predators

Internet predators use online communication to build up trust so they can try to get a potential victim to meet with them in person. To avoid falling victim to Internet predators, follow these guidelines for online safety.

Avoid sending photos to strangers online. In addition, be sure to get permission from a trusted adult before sending photos to friends.

Avoid responding to inappropriate messages. If anyone sends you a message that makes you feel uncomfortable for any reason, tell a parent or other trusted adult. You can also report the person to your internet provider.

Be cautious about meeting an online friend. If you decide to meet, do it in a public place with a trusted adult present.

Talk to a trusted adult. Feeling uncomfortable or scared about something that happened online? Tell a trusted adult about it immediately.

Although you can hide some information, it may not be completely private.

>>> **Reading Check**

LIST *What are three things you can do to protect yourself from online predators?*

Understanding Privacy Settings

Many social media networks and other websites have privacy settings. Privacy settings allow you to control who reads and comments on your personal pages and profiles. However, it is important to understand how each site's settings work.

Although you may be able to hide some information, such as your phone number, or address, it may not be completely hidden. For example, if a friend posts a comment on your page or personal website that includes your address or current location, another person can read the post and find out where you are or what even your address.

Most websites prompt you to read a privacy statement before you sign up. Always read the website's privacy statements. Review the privacy settings page whenever changes are made to the website. Remember to think about the information you post to a website or blog. Even if you delete the information or pictures, a copy will stay on the Internet. People with knowledge of the Internet can find the pictures or information even after it is deleted. It is easier not to post information than to try and remove it after it is posted.

>>> **Reading Check**

EXPLAIN *Why is it important to understand a website's privacy settings?* ■

REVIEW

>>> **After You Read**

1. **DEFINE** Define *personal safety*.
2. **DESCRIBE** What strategies should you use to keep yourself safe if you are walking home alone?
3. **IDENTIFY** If you were approached by a stranger on the Internet, how would you protect yourself?

>>> **Thinking Critically**

4. **APPLY** Imagine that you are home alone and a stranger comes to the door. He tells you that he needs help and asks if he can use your phone. What should you do to avoid risks to your safety?
5. **EVALUATE** Greg has been at a friend's house all day. Now, it is dark outside and he is uncomfortable walking home alone. What could Greg do?

>>> **Applying Health Skills**

6. **COMMUNICATION SKILLS** Erica has been chatting with a stranger online. At first the messages were harmless, but now she is uncomfortable with the conversations. Write a short dialogue that your friend could use to tell her parents about this issue.

 Review

 Audio

Weather Safety *and* Natural Disasters

BIG IDEA Early warning signs give time to plan and stay safe during weather emergencies and natural disasters.

Before You Read

QUICK WRITE What is one kind of weather emergency that is common in your area? List two things you could do to stay safe during that emergency.

 Video

As You Read

STUDY ORGANIZER Make the study organizer on page 54 to record the information presented in Lesson 5.

Vocabulary

› weather emergency
› tornado
› hurricane
› blizzard
› frostbite
› natural disaster
› earthquake
› aftershocks

 Audio

 Bilingual Glossary

©2010 Willoughby Owen/Getty Images

Myth vs. Fact

Myth: The area under a highway overpass provides shelter from a tornado.
Fact: You should seek shelter in a building. If there are no buildings, lie down in a ditch and cover your head with your hands. If you cannot exit the vehicle, leave your seat belt on and put your head down below the windows. Cover your head and body with a blanket, if possible.

WHAT ARE WEATHER EMERGENCIES?

MAIN IDEA Weather emergencies are dangerous situations brought on by changes in the atmosphere.

Weather events make the news on a fairly regular basis. These events often happen with little warning. People cannot prevent them. A weather emergency is *a dangerous situation brought on by changes in the atmosphere.* Weather emergencies are natural events. Examples include thunderstorms, tornadoes, hurricanes, and blizzards.

Weather emergencies can impact a person's safety and health. As a result, the National Weather Service (NWS) works to track the progress of storms and sends out bulletins to the public. The bulletins keep people informed about possible weather emergencies. This helps keep people and communities safe.

Storm bulletins may involve watches or warnings. A storm watch indicates that a storm is likely to develop. A storm warning indicates that a severe storm has already developed and a weather emergency is happening. If your area is under a storm warning, turn on the television or radio. Follow the instructions of the NWS and local officials.

Weather emergencies can **impact** a person's *safety* and *health.*

Technology has helped scientists who watch the weather. Satellites gather data very quickly and feed it into powerful computers. Computers can also help predict the paths of storms. Television and the Internet can warn the public of danger very quickly. These early warnings give people more time to plan and stay safe.

Thunderstorms *and* Lightning

How can you protect yourself during thunderstorms? Whenever you see lightning or hear thunder, seek shelter and stay there. Do not use the telephone, unless it is a cordless or cell phone. Be prepared for a power loss. If you are outdoors, look for the nearest building. An alternative is an enclosed metal vehicle with the windows completely shut. If you are in an open field with no shelter nearby, lie down. Wait for the storm to pass. Avoid all metal objects including electric wires, fences, machinery, motors, and power tools. Unsafe places include underneath canopies, small picnic or rain shelters, or near trees.

Tornadoes

A tornado is a *whirling, funnel-shaped windstorm that drops from storm clouds to the ground.* If a tornado watch is issued for your area, listen to the radio for updates. Prepare to take shelter if you need to protect yourself. If a tornado warning is issued for your area, move to the shelter immediately.

You are safest underground in a cellar or basement. If you cannot go underground, take shelter in an inner hallway or any central, windowless room such as a bathroom or closet. If you are outdoors, lie in a ditch or flat on the ground. Stay away from trees, cars, and anything that could fall on you.

If you are in a room with furniture, stay under a heavy table. Lying in a bathtub under a cushion, mattress, or blanket may also offer good protection.

Hurricanes

A hurricane is *a strong windstorm with driving rain that forms over the sea.* Hurricanes occur in coastal regions.

Weather experts track the path of a hurricane by recording the coordinates of its location at regular intervals. *Describe how tracking a hurricane might help people who live in a coastal area.*

The National Weather Service tracks hurricanes and can estimate when and where a hurricane will hit land. This gives people time to plan ahead. Take the following steps to stay safe during a hurricane.

Before the hurricane arrives, secure your home. Board up windows. Close storm shutters before the winds start blowing.

Bring inside items such as furniture and bikes that wind could pick up and smash into houses.

Stay alert to TV or radio reports. Sometimes residents will be instructed to leave their homes, or evacuate, and head inland. It is necessary to follow these safety instructions. If no evacuation is ordered, stay indoors. Avoid standing near windows and doors.

Blizzards

Do you live in an area hit by snow in the winter? If you do, you may have experienced a blizzard, *a very heavy snowstorm with winds up to 45 miles per hour.* Protect yourself during blizzards and winter storms by following these precautions:

Stay indoors. The safest place during a blizzard is inside. Visibility is reduced during a blizzard, making it easy to get lost or disoriented if walking outside or even in a car.

Bundle up. A leading danger in a blizzard is hypothermia. Another health risk is frostbite, or *freezing of the skin.* Frostbite can cause severe injury to the skin and deeper tissues. If you must go out, wear layers of loose-fitting lightweight clothing under layers of outerwear that is both wind- and waterproof. Add a scarf, hat, gloves and boots.

> ›› **Reading Check**
>
> RECALL *What are three ways to stay safe during a blizzard?*

WHAT ARE NATURAL DISASTERS?

MAIN IDEA Natural disasters are dramatic events caused by Earth's processes.

Like weather emergencies, natural disasters can cause serious health and safety problems. A **natural disaster** is *an event caused by nature that results in widespread damage.* Natural disasters include floods and earthquakes. One way to stay safe during a natural disaster is to plan ahead. Keep some basic supplies on hand such as fresh water, a radio, a flashlight, batteries, blankets, canned food, a can opener, and a first-aid kit.

Floods

Floods can occur almost anywhere. Hurricanes and heavy rainfall can cause floods.

Flash floods, floods that occur with little or no warning, are the most dangerous of all. Flashflood waters rise very quickly and are surprisingly powerful. Two feet of moving water has enough force to sweep away cars. Water levels higher than two feet can carry away trucks and houses.

Two feet of moving water has enough force to sweep away cars.

If the NWS issues a flood watch for your area, take your emergency kit, and go to the highest place in your home. Listen to a battery-powered radio for a flood warning.

If a flood warning is issued and you are told to evacuate, do so immediately. The following tips can help you survive a flood:

- Head for higher ground. If it is possible to travel safely, go to the home of a relative or neighbor who lives outside the warning area.
- Avoid walking, swimming, riding a bike, or driving a car through flooding water. You could be swept away, electrocuted by downed power lines, or drown.
- Drink only bottled water. Floodwater carries harmful pathogens that can make you sick. Flood water is easily polluted by trash and other waste.
- If you have evacuated the area, return home only after you are told it is safe for you to do so. Returning home before the authorities give the all-clear can put you at risk. It may also break the law.
- Make sure that everything that came in contact with the floodwater is cleaned and disinfected. Wear rubber or latex gloves during the cleanup. Throw out all food that may have become contaminated or if refrigeration was lost during the flood. Make sure the water supply is safe before drinking water.

> **Reading Check**
>
> **EXPLAIN** *Why are flashfloods dangerous?*

Health SKILLS ACTIVITY

Practicing Healthful Behaviors

Creating an *Emergency Supplies Kit*

An emergency supplies kit should include enough supplies to last for three days. If you evacuate your home, take these supplies plus walking shoes, money, and medicines.

* **GALLON JUGS OF FRESH WATER.** Allow one gallon of fresh water per person per day.

* **CANNED FOOD, CAN OPENER, AND UTENSILS**

* **FIRST-AID KIT**

* **BATTERY-POWERED OR CRANK-POWERED RADIO, FLASHLIGHT, AND SPARE BATTERIES**

Create your own emergency supplies kit. Prepare an emergency plan to follow in case of an emergency.

Earthquakes

An **earthquake** is *a shifting of the earth's plates, resulting in a shaking of Earth's surface.* Earthquakes usually involve more than a single event. A large quake typically is followed by a series of aftershocks. **Aftershocks** are *smaller earthquakes as the earth readjusts after the main earthquake.* Collapsing walls and falling debris cause most injuries in an earthquake. To reduce your risk of injury from an earthquake, follow these precautions:

• **Stay indoors.** Crouch under heavy furniture. Stay away from objects that might fall, shatter, or cave in.

• **Get in the open if outdoors.** Avoid buildings, trees, power lines, streetlights, and overpasses.

• **Be careful afterward.** Stay out of damaged buildings. Damaged electrical and gas lines could be hazardous.

Scientists cannot predict when and where an earthquake will strike. However, they can measure how strong earthquakes are when they happen. The Richter scale rates the force of ground motion during an earthquake. An earthquake that measures 1 on this scale is slight. One that measures a 2 is 10 times stronger than 1. Likewise, one that measures a 3 is 10 times stronger than 2, and so on.

The most destructive earthquakes have a magnitude of 7 or more on the Richter scale. They are much less common. Scientists have never recorded an earthquake that measures more than 9 on the Richter scale.

During an earthquake, stay clear of falling objects.

Name two ways to stay safe during an earthquake.

Get under a sturdy piece of furniture. Cover your head with your arms or a pillow.

Stay away from windows, mirrors, and other objects that might shatter.

Stay away from trees, buildings, and power lines. They may fall.

Stay away from tall or heavy objects that could fall on you.

Find a clear, open area. Drop to the ground and protect your head with your arms. To do so, clasp your hands together at the back of your head, and bring your elbows together in front of your face.

REVIEW

>>> **After You Read**

1. **DEFINE** Define *hurricane*, and use it in a sentence.
2. **DESCRIBE** Tell how to protect yourself during a flood.
3. **COMPARE** What is the difference between a weather emergency and a natural disaster?

>>> **Thinking Critically**

4. **APPLY** You are playing soccer in a field, and you see a flash of lightning from an approaching thunderstorm. What should you do?
5. **SYNTHESIZE** After a major earthquake, your friend wants you go with him to inspect a damaged building. How would you respond? Explain your answer.

>>> **Applying Health Skills**

6. **COMMUNICATION SKILLS** With a partner, choose a weather emergency from this lesson. Write and perform a skit to demonstrate strategies for staying safe during that event.

Review

Audio

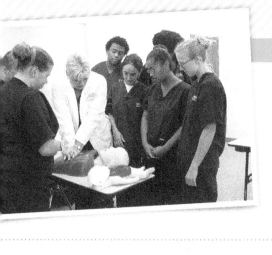

First Aid *and* Emergencies

BIG IDEA Knowing how to administer basic first aid can save a person's life in an emergency.

Before You Read

QUICK WRITE Write a couple of sentences describing how you would treat a minor burn.

▶ Video

As You Read

STUDY ORGANIZER Make the study organizer on page 54 to record the information presented in Lesson 6.

Vocabulary

> first aid
> universal precautions
> abdominal thrust
> cardiopulmonary resuscitation (CPR)
> rescue breathing
> fracture
> dislocation

 Audio

🔤 Bilingual Glossary

McGraw-Hill Companies, Inc. Jan L. Saeger, photographer

Developing Good Character

Citizenship A good neighbor and citizen is prepared to report accidents, fires, serious illnesses, injuries, and crimes. Familiarize yourself with emergency phone numbers to call in your community. Make a list to keep handy by the telephone.

GIVING FIRST AID

MAIN IDEA First aid is the immediate care given to someone who becomes injured or ill until regular medical care can be provided.

Dania was taking a walk in her neighborhood when she saw someone lying on the ground. The man was wearing a bicycle helmet. A bicycle was lying nearby. Dania gently touched his shoulder and said, "Are you alright?" The man did not respond. Dania immediately pulled out her cell phone and dialed 911.

Some emergencies are minor. You cut your fingertip and it bleeds. A friend falls while skateboarding and injures his or her knee. These types of minor injuries should be cleaned with soap and warm water. They may also be wrapped or covered with a breathable bandage.

You can *prevent* further **injury** and may even *speed recovery* if you **know what to do** in an emergency.

Other emergencies can be life-threatening. Taking immediate action can mean the difference between life and death. **First aid** is *the immediate care given to someone who becomes injured or ill until regular medical care can be provided.*

Knowing basic first aid may help you deal with some emergencies while you wait for help to arrive. You can prevent further injury and may even speed recovery if you know what to do in an emergency. Knowing what *not* to do is equally important. Anyone who has received first aid should be taken to a medical provider as soon as possible.

Steps *to* Take *in* an Emergency

How can you tell if an emergency is life-threatening? A person's life is considered in danger if he or she: (1) has stopped breathing, (2) has no heartbeat, (3) is bleeding severely, (4) is choking, (5) has swallowed poison, or (6) has been severely burned. These situations require immediately help. Call 911. Next, begin to treat the person. Proper training is needed to give first aid. In an emergency, the American Red Cross suggests the following strategy: Check-Call-Care.

Check the scene and the victim. Often something you see, hear, or smell will alert you to an emergency. Is someone calling out in trouble? Have you heard glass shattering? Do you smell smoke or anything unusual that makes your eyes sting or causes you to cough or have difficulty breathing? These sensations can signal a chemical spill or toxic gas release. Make sure the area is safe for you and the victim.

Move the person only if he or she is in danger of additional injury.

Call for help. Call 911 or the local EMS number. *EMS* stands for "emergency medical service." When making a call for help, stay calm. Describe the emergency to the operator and give a street address or describe the location by using landmarks. The operator will notify the police, fire, or emergency medical service departments. Stay on the phone until the operator tells you to hang up.

How can you tell if an *emergency* is **life-threatening?**

Care for the person until help arrives. After you have called for help, stay with the person until help arrives.

When someone is injured, giving first aid can help prevent further injury and possibly speed recovery. *What is first aid?*

Loosen any tight clothing on the person's body. Use a coat or blanket to keep the person warm or provide shade if the weather is warm. This will help maintain a normal body temperature. Avoid moving the person to prevent further pain or injury. Only move the person if he or she is in danger, such as in the path of traffic. Hands-Only™ Cardiopulmonary Resuscitation (CPR) may be necessary if the person is unconscious and unresponsive.

Universal Precautions

Viruses such as HIV, hepatitis B, and hepatitis C can be spread through contact with an infected person's blood. As a result, steps should be taken to minimize contact with another person's blood. To protect yourself when giving first aid, follow universal precautions, or *actions taken to prevent the spread of disease by treating all blood as if it were contaminated.* Wear protective gloves while treating someone. If possible, use a facemask or shield, when giving first aid for breathing emergencies. Cover any open wounds on your body with sterile dressings. Avoid touching any object that was in contact with the person's blood. Always wash hands thoroughly after giving first aid.

>> **Reading Check**

EXPLAIN *What information should you give when calling 911 or another emergency number?*

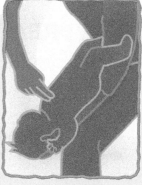
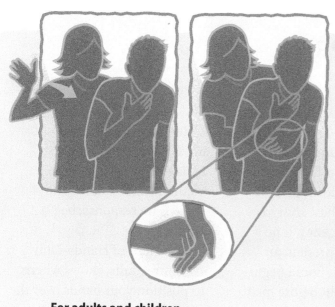

For adults and children

① Give 5 back blows with the heel of your hand.

② Place the thumb of your fist against the person's abdomen, just above the navel. Grasp your fist with your other hand. Give quick, inward and upward thrusts until the person coughs up the object. If the person becomes unconscious, call 911 or the local emergency number. Begin CPR.

For infants

① Hold the infant facedown on your forearm. Support the child's head and neck with your hand. Point the head downward so that it is lower than the chest. With the heel of your free hand, give the child five blows between the shoulder blades. If the child doesn't cough up the object, move on to chest thrusts (step 2).

② Turn the infant over onto his or her back. Support the head with one hand. With two or three fingers, press into the middle of the child's breastbone—directly between and just below the nipples—five times. Repeat chest thrusts until the object comes out or the infant begins to breathe, cry, or cough. Make sure a health care professional checks the infant. If the infant becomes unconscious, call 911.

FIRST AID FOR CHOKING

MAIN IDEA Abdominal thrusts can help save someone who is choking.

If a person is clutching his or her throat, that is the universal sign for choking. Symptoms of choking include gasping or wheezing, a reddish-purple coloration, bulging eyes, and an inability to speak.

If a person can speak or cough, it is not a choking emergency. However, if the choking person makes no sound and cannot speak or cough, give first aid immediately.

If an adult or child is choking, give the person five blows to the back. Stand slightly behind the person who is choking.

Place one of your arms diagonally across the person's chest and lean him or her forward. Strike the person between the shoulder blades five times. If this does not dislodge the object, give five abdominal thrusts. An **abdominal thrust** is a *quick inward and upward pull into the diaphragm to force an obstruction out of the airway.*

If an infant is choking, hold the infant face down along your forearm, using your thigh for support. Give five back blows between the shoulder blades.

Follow these steps to help a person who is choking. *Why do you think chest thrusts are used to help a choking infant?*

If this does not dislodge the object, turn the infant over and perform five chest thrusts with your fingers to force an object out of the airway.

If you are alone and choking, give yourself an abdominal thrust. Make a fist and position it slightly above your navel. With your other hand, grasp your fist and thrust inward and upward into your abdomen until the object dislodges. You can also lean over the back of a chair, or any firm object, pressing your abdomen into it.

RESCUE BREATHING AND CPR

All organs need oxygen-rich blood. If the heart stops beating, the flow of blood to the brain stops, too. When the brain stops functioning, breathing also stops. If you are confident that the victim is not breathing, it is necessary to begin **cardiopulmonary resuscitation** (CPR)—*a first-aid procedure to restore breathing and circulation.*

The American Heart Association (AHA) recommends two forms of CPR. A trained person will perform CPR that combines chest compressions with **rescue breathing,** *a first aid procedure where someone forces air into the lungs of a person who cannot breathe on his or her own.* A person who is untrained in giving CPR can perform *Hands-Only™ CPR.* This form of CPR focuses only on chest compressions. In an emergency, if no trained person is present, an untrained person should begin Hands-Only™ CPR before medical professionals arrive.

Hands-Only™ CPR *for* Adults

The first step is to call 911. Before performing CPR, tap the victim and shout, "Are you OK?" Check the victim for signs of normal breathing. Put your ear and cheek close to the victim's nose and mouth.

Listen and feel for exhaled air. Look to see if the chest is rising and falling. If the victim is unconscious and there is no response, begin Hands-Only™ CPR.

The Steps of Hands-Only™ CPR for Adults, shows where to position your hands over the victim's chest and begin compressions. Try to give 100 chest compressions each minute, until the victim responds or until paramedics arrive.

Follow these steps to help a person whose heart has stopped beating. *In what type of situation should you use CPR?*

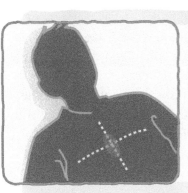

1. Use your fingers to find the end of the victim's sternum (breastbone), where the ribs come together.
2. Place two fingers over the end of the sternum.
3. Place the heel of your other hand against the sternum, directly above your fingers (on the side closest to the victim's face).
4. Place your other hand on top of the one you just put in position. Interlock the fingers of your hands and raise your fingers so they do not touch the person's chest.

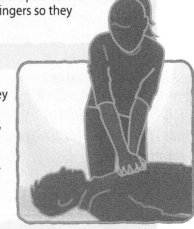

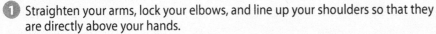

1. Straighten your arms, lock your elbows, and line up your shoulders so that they are directly above your hands.
2. Press downward firmly on the person's chest, forcing the breastbone down by 1.5 to 2 inches (3.8 to 5 cm).
3. Begin compressions at a steady pace. You can maintain a rhythm by counting. "One and two and three and…" Press down each time you say a number. Emergency medical experts recommend pressing down 100 times a minute.

FIRST AID FOR SEVERE BLEEDING

MAIN IDEA To control bleeding, apply a cloth and direct pressure to the wound and elevate the wound, if possible.

When providing first aid to a person who is bleeding severely, follow universal precautions. Avoid touching the person's blood or wear gloves. Always wash your hands when you are finished. If the person has a wound that is bleeding severely or needs other medical help, call 911. Wash the wound with mild soap and water to remove dirt and debris. Follow these steps to control the bleeding:

- Raise the wounded body part above the level of the heart.
- Cover the wound with sterile gauze or a clean cloth. Apply steady pressure to the wound for five minutes, or until help arrives. Do not stop to check the wound.
- If blood soaks through the gauze, add another gauze pad on top of the first and continue to apply pressure.
- Once the bleeding slows, secure the pad in place with a bandage or strips of gauze. The pad should be snug.
- Stay with the victim until help arrives.

FIRST AID FOR BURNS

MAIN IDEA Major burns require medical attention as soon as possible.

A **first-degree burn,** or *superficial burn,* is a burn in which only the outer layer of skin has burned. There may be pain and swelling. Flush the burned area with cold water for at least 20 minutes. Loosely wrap the burn in a clean, dry dressing.

A **second-degree burn,** or *partial-thickness burn,* is a moderately serious burn in which the burned area blisters.

There is usually severe pain and swelling. Flush the burned area with cold water for at least 20 minutes. Do not use ice. Elevate the burned area. Loosely wrap the cooled burn in a clean, dry dressing. Do not pop blisters or peel loose skin. If the burn is larger than 2 or 3 inches in diameter, or is on the hands, feet, face, groin, buttocks, or a major joint, get medical help immediately.

A **third-degree burn,** or *full-thickness burn,* is a very serious burn in which all the layers of skin are damaged. There may be little or no pain felt at this stage. They usually result from fire, electricity, or chemicals. Call 911 immediately. Do not remove burned clothing. Cover the area with a cool, clean, moist cloth. Only a medical professional should treat full-thickness burns.

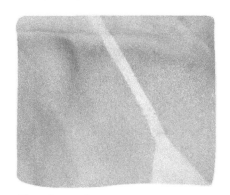

First-degree burn

Second-degree burn

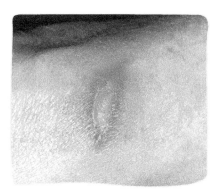

Third-degree burn

FIRST AID FOR OTHER EMERGENCIES

MAIN IDEA Animal bites, bruises and sprains, broken or dislocated bones and poisonings require different types of treatment.

Other common emergencies that you may encounter include insect and animal bites, bruises and sprains, broken or dislocated bones, and poisonings.

Insect *and* Animal Bites

Insect bites and stings can be painful but are not usually dangerous unless the person is allergic to the venom of the insect. If an allergic person has been stung, get medical help immediately. For all other bites and stings follow these steps:

- Remove the stinger by scraping it off with a firm, straight-edged object. Do not use tweezers.
- Wash the site thoroughly with mild soap and water.
- Apply ice (wrapped in a cloth) to the site for ten minutes to reduce pain and swelling. Continue to apply ice, alternating ten minutes on and off.

- To treat animal bites, wash the bite with soap and water. Apply pressure to stop any bleeding. Apply antibiotic ointment and a sterile dressing. For any bite that has broken the skin, contact your doctor.

If an allergic person has been *stung*, **get medical help** immediately.

Bruises *and* Sprains

A bruise forms when an impact breaks blood vessels below the surface of the skin. This allows blood to leak from the vessels into the tissues under the skin, leaving a black or bluish mark. A sprain is a condition in which the ligaments that hold the joints in position are stretched or torn. Symptoms of sprains include swelling and bruising.

While a doctor should evaluate serious sprains, minor sprains can be treated using the P.R.I.C.E. method:
- **Protect** the injured part by keeping it still. Moving it could cause further injury.
- **Rest** the affected joint for 24 to 48 hours.
- **Ice** the injured part to reduce swelling and pain. A cloth between the skin and ice bag will reduce discomfort. Be sure to remove the ice every 15–20 minutes so that it does not become too cold.
- **Compress** the injured area by wrapping it in an elastic bandage.
- **Elevate** the injured part above the level of the heart to reduce swelling.

Ice helps slow swelling after a sprain. *How can you reduce the risk of sprains during physical activity?*

McGraw-Hill Companies, Inc. Rick Brady, photographer

Broken *or* Dislocated Bones

A **fracture** is *a break in a bone.* Fractures usually happen along the length of a bone. An open fracture is a complete break with one or both sides of the bone piercing the skin. A closed fracture does not break the skin and may be difficult to identify. Pain, swelling and a misshapen appearance are typical symptoms of a closed fracture. However, not all broken bones cause immediate pain. An X ray is the only method to confirm that a bone is broken.

Problems can also develop where bones meet at a joint. A **dislocation** is *a major injury that happens when a bone is forced from its normal position within a joint.* For example, if your upper arm bone is pulled out of your shoulder socket, it is dislocated. Moving a broken bone or dislocated joint could cause further injury. For both fractures and dislocations, call for help at once. While you wait for help, keep the victim still. Once a trained medical professional arrives, he or she can then immobilize the fracture or dislocation.

Poisoning

A poison is a substance that causes harm when swallowed, inhaled, absorbed by the skin, or injected into the body. Medicines and household products play a role in about half of all poisonings. All poisonings require immediate treatment.

In the event of a poisoning, call 911 or the nearest poison control center. Be ready to provide information about the victim and the suspected poison. The poison control center will advise you about how to proceed. Keep the person warm and breathing. Look for extra traces of poison around the victim's mouth. Remove these with a damp, clean cloth wrapped around your finger. Save the container of poison. and show it to the emergency medical care providers.

Medicines and **household products** play a role in about half of all *poisonings.*

If a poisonous chemical has made contact with someone's skin, remove all clothing that has touched the chemical and rinse the skin with water for 15 minutes. Wash with soap and water. Call the poison control center while the skin is being washed.

Some cases of poisoning are caused by contact with a poisonous plant. Poison ivy, poison oak, and poison sumac are three such plants. Most of these injuries can be treated at home using soap and water and over-the counter creams. For severe cases, see a doctor for treatment.

> ## Reading Check
>
> **LIST** *Give two ways poisons can enter the body.* ■

>> **LESSON 6**

REVIEW

>>> After You Read

1. **VOCABULARY** Define *first aid.* Use the term in a sentence.
2. **RECALL** Name four universal precautions to take when administering first aid.
3. **LIST** Briefly give the steps in controlling severe bleeding.

>>> Thinking Critically

4. **INFER** Why can you infer that a person who cannot speak or cough is choking?
5. **APPLY** If you come upon an injured person on a hiking trail, should you try to move the person off the trail? Why or why not?

>>> Applying Health Skills

6. **STRESS MANAGEMENT** Emergency situations are often very stressful. With classmates, discuss strategies for reducing stress while dealing with a medical emergency.

 Review

🔊 Audio

Hands-On HEALTH ACTIVITY

A Home Emergency Kit

WHAT YOU WILL NEED
* one piece of poster board
* marker
* paper
* pencil or pen

WHAT YOU WILL DO

1 Working in a small group, brainstorm all of the supplies you would include in a home emergency kit. Your kit should include enough items to last for three days.

2 Have one member of the group write all the items on the poster board.

3 Discuss why you feel certain items should or should not be included.

4 Make your list final. Then, compare your list with other groups in the class. Are your lists similar? How are they different?

WRAPPING IT UP

Write down the final list on a piece of paper. At home, discuss creating a home emergency kit with your family using the list you created.

Weather emergencies and natural disasters are situations that no one can prevent. You can, however, be prepared. Creating a home emergency kit for your family can help keep you safe and secure until the emergency is over.

McGraw-Hill Companies, Inc. Ken Karp, photographer

READING REVIEW

FOLDABLES and Other Study Aids

Take out the Foldable® that you created for Lesson 1 and any study organizers that you created for Lessons 2-6. Find a partner and quiz each other using these study aids.

LESSON 1 Building Safe Habits

BIG IDEA Being safety conscious means being aware that safety is important and acting safely.

- Accidents and accidental injuries can affect people of all ages.
- For any accident to occur, three elements must be present.

LESSON 2 Safety at Home and School

BIG IDEA Following safety rules can keep you safe both at home and away from home.

- Your home may be filled with many potential safety hazards, such as stairs or appliances.
- It is a healthy practice to have a fire safety plan, fire extinguisher, and working smoke alarms.
- Following rules at school helps you, other students, and teachers stay safe.

LESSON 3 Safety on the Road and Outdoors

BIG IDEA Following safety rules can help prevent injury on the road and outdoors.

- Safety in vehicles includes wearing a safety belt and not distracting the driver.
- Safety precautions make outdoor activities more fun.

LESSON 4 Personal Safety and Online Safety

BIG IDEA You can protect yourself from violence by avoiding dangerous situations.

- You can reduce your risk of becoming a victim of violence by avoiding unsafe situations.
- Staying safe online is an important part of your overall safety.

LESSON 5 Weather Safety and Natural Disasters

BIG IDEA Weather emergencies include thunderstorms, tornadoes, hurricanes, and blizzards. Natural disasters include floods and earthquakes.

- Weather emergencies are dangerous situations brought on by changes in the atmosphere.
- Natural disasters are dramatic events caused by Earth's processes.

LESSON 6 First Aid and Emergencies

BIG IDEA Knowing how to administer basic first aid can save a person's life in an emergency.

- First aid is the immediate care given to someone who becomes injured or ill until regular medical care can be provided.
- Abdominal thrusts can save someone who is choking.
- Hands-Only™ CPR is for older children and adults who have stopped breathing.
- To control bleeding, apply a cloth and direct pressure to the wound and elevate the limb, if possible.
- Major burns require medical attention.
- Animal bites, bruises and sprains, broken or dislocated bones and poisonings require different treatments.

 Review

 Web Quest

ASSESSMENT

Reviewing Vocabulary *and* Main Ideas

› hazards 　　　　› defensive driving 　　　› fire extinguisher 　　› accident chain
› flammable 　　　› accident 　　　　　　　› hypothermia 　　　　› electrical overload

On a sheet of paper, write the numbers 1–8. After each number, write the term from the list that best completes each sentence.

LESSON 1 **Building Safe Habits**

1. A(n) _____ is any event that was not intended to happen.

2. _____ are potential sources of danger.

3. A(n) _____ is a series of events that include a situation, an unsafe habit, and an unsafe action.

LESSON 2 **Safety at Home and School**

4. A(n) _____ can be used to put out a grease fire.

5. Materials that are _____ are able to catch fire easily.

6. _____ is a dangerous situation in which too much electric current flows along a single circuit.

LESSON 3 **Safety on the Road and Outdoors**

7. _____ involves watching out for other people on the road and anticipating unsafe acts.

8. When outside in cold weather, it is best to wear layers to reduce the risk of _____.

On a sheet of paper, write the numbers 9–16. Write *True* or *False* for each statement below. If the statement is false, change the underlined word or phrase to make it true.

LESSON 4 **Personal Safety and Online Safety**

9. <u>Personal safety</u> is the steps you take to prevent yourself from becoming the victim of a crime.

10. Precautions are actions taken <u>after</u> an event to prevent harm.

LESSON 5 **Weather Safety and Natural Disasters**

11. The center of a hurricane is called the <u>eye.</u>

12. In a tornado, you are safest <u>underground</u>.

LESSON 6 **First Aid and Emergencies**

13. A <u>sprain</u> is an invisible break in a bone.

14. A <u>third-degree burn</u> damages all layers of skin.

15. The abdominal thrusts maneuver is used to help a victim of <u>shock</u>.

16. <u>Gasping</u> is the universal sign for choking.

eAssessment

Using complete sentences, answer the following questions on a sheet of paper.

 *Thinking* **Critically**

17. EVALUATE How would you assess whether a person needed CPR?

18. ANALYZE How does an understanding of accident chains help prevent injuries?

 *Write* **About It**

19. NARRATIVE WRITING Write a short story about a teen involved in a situation that leads to an accident. Describe the situation and the events that make up the accident chain. Then write an alternate ending describing how the teen used strategies to prevent the accident from happening.

 STANDARDIZED TEST PRACTICE

Writing

Read the paragraph below. Write a short essay about other places that you think automatic external defibrillators should be placed to save people who are having heart attacks. Explain your choices.

CPR can save the lives of people having a heart attack. However, public access to automatic external defibrillators (AEDs) can save even more. AEDs are machines that detect an irregular or missing heartbeat. When the machine detects something is wrong, it sends an electric shock through the chest that restarts the heart. In the past, all hospitals had AEDs. Today, some cities are beginning to place them in areas where the public can easily access them.

City officials are also training people on how to use the AEDs. One city trained police to use AEDs, and every police car now carries one of these machines. In that city, the survival rate for people having heart attacks rose from 28 percent to 40 percent. Many airports and airplanes have AEDs that have already saved people's lives. The more AEDs that are available, the more lives they can save.

KEEPING SAFE—AT HOME AND ELSEWHERE

The first step in staying safe is being safety conscious.

FIRE

It is a healthy practice to have:
- A fire escape plan
- A fire extinguisher
- Working smoke alarms

ON THE WEB

- Don't give out personal information.
- Keep passwords private.
- Don't send photos to strangers.
- Don't respond to inappropriate messages.
- If you want to meet an online friend, do so in a public place with a trusted adult present.
- Remember to think before you post!

PREVENTING FALLS

Most falls in the home occur in the kitchen, the bathroom, or on the stairs.

Bathroom
- Put a nonskid mat near the tub or shower.
- Use rugs that have a rubber backing to prevent the rug from slipping.

Rubber

Staircase
- Keep staircases well lit and clear of objects.
- Apply nonslip treads to stairs.
- Make sure handrails are secure.

PREVENT POISONING
- Make sure medications are in containers with childproof caps.
- Avoid referring to children's medicine as candy.
- Store medications out of the reach of children.

ELECTRICITY
- Never use an electrical appliance around water.
- Unplug electrical appliances when they are not in use.
- Avoid running cords under rugs.
- Cover unused outlets with plastic protectors.

Kitchen
- Clean up spills right away.
- Use a stepstool to get items that are out of reach.

ON FOOT
- Walk on the sidewalk if there is one.
- If there is no sidewalk, walk facing oncoming traffic, staying to the left side of the road.
- Avoid talking on a cell phone or wearing headphones as you walk.

ON WHEELS
- Wear a helmet, wrist guards, elbow pads, and knee pads.
- Avoid riding on wet, dirty, or uneven surfaces.

KEEPING THE ENVIRONMENT SAFE

Many activities can pollute the environment and make it harmful for for all living things.

ACID RAIN

Sulfur dioxide and nitrogen oxides are produced when fossil fuels are burned. They mix with moisture in the air to form acid rain. Over time, acid rain can:
- harm plants and whole forests.
- contaminate water supplies.
- eat away at rock and stone.

AIR POLLUTION

The main cause of air pollution is the burning of fossil fuels. Energy from fossil fuels provides heat for homes, electricity to power factories and cities, and power to most motor vehicles. Fossils fuels are:
- oil
- coal
- natural gas

SMOG

Smog is a yellow-brown haze that forms when sunlight mixes with gases formed by burning fossil fuels.

DAMAGE TO THE OZONE LAYER

The ozone layer provides protection from the sun. Without it, people are more likely to develop skin cancer and eye damage. Chemicals that damage the ozone layer can be found in :
- aerosol cans
- refrigerators
- air conditioners
- automobile emissions

GLOBAL WARMING

The trapping of heat by carbon dioxide and other gases in the air is known as the greenhouse effect. This may be the cause of global warming, or a rise in Earth's temperatures. Global warming can affect weather patterns and ocean water levels.

How can you help?

- Walk or ride your bike.
- Use public transportation or carpool.
- Stay tobacco free.
- Plant trees and other plants.
- Don't burn trash, leaves, and brush.

WATER POLLUTION

Water is vital to all forms of life. However, wastes, chemicals, and other harmful substances pollute Earth's water. Water pollution is a widespread problem. Forty percent of all the nation's rivers, lakes, streams, and estuaries, or coastal waters, are too polluted to use for swimming, fishing, or drinking.

 Sewage
 Garbage
 Detergents
 Other household waste
 Chemicals

How can you help?

- Pick up pet waste from public areas to reduce toxic runoff.
- Use soaps, detergents, and cleaners that are biodegradable.
- Pick up any litter that is not hazardous.
- Dispose of chemicals properly and legally. Never pour them into a drain.
    - Take hazardous waste materials to the appropriate collection sites.

Green Schools + Environmental Health

LESSONS

 PREMIUM ONLINE RESOURCES 〉

 Audio   Videos   Bilingual Glossary

 Fitness Zone  Web Quest   Review

Picking up trash is one way to keep the environment clean. *How do you keep the environment clean in your neighborhood?*

37

Pollution *and* Health

> **BIG IDEA** Pollution harms the environment and your health, and is often ugly.

Before You Read

QUICK WRITE Give three examples of pollution that affect your local community.

 Video

As You Read

FOLDABLES Study Organizer

Make the Foldable® on page 55 to record the information presented in Lesson 1.

Vocabulary

> environment
> pollute
> pollution
> fossil fuels
> acid rain
> ozone
> smog
> ozone layer
> greenhouse effect
> global warming
> sewage

 Audio

 Bilingual Glossary

Myth vs. Fact

Myth Carbon dioxide is the only gas that causes global warming.

Fact Gases such as methane and fluorinated gases also contribute to global warming. These gases are referred to as High Global Warming Potential gases.

YOUR ENVIRONMENT

> **MAIN IDEA** Pollution is made up of dirty or harmful substances in the environment.

Vivian has been in the habit of turning on the television as soon as she gets home. She leaves it on, even when she isn't watching it. Lately, she has been wondering how much electricity she is wasting by doing this - and how much air pollution she might be causing. She decides to change her habit and turn off the television when she leaves the room.

Your **environment** is *all the living and nonliving things around you.* The environment includes forests, mountains, rivers, and oceans. It also includes your home, school, and community. The air you breathe, the water you drink, the plants and animals that live nearby, and the climate are all part of the environment. All living things are affected by the environment.

It's *important* for **each person** to *do* his or her part to **keep the** *environment* **clean.**

Sometimes people pollute the environment. To **pollute** means *to make unfit or harmful for living things.* The result is **pollution,** *dirty or harmful substances in the environment.* Pollution can harm your health. It affects everything in your environment. On days when air pollution is high, you may hear news reports suggesting that people with breathing problems limit the time they spend outside. Our health depends on a healthy environment. It's important for each person to do his or her part to keep the environment clean.

> **Reading Check**
>
> **IDENTIFY** *What is pollution?*

PhotoAlto/Getty Images

AIR POLLUTION

The leading cause of air pollution is the burning of fossil fuels. **Fossil** (FAH·suhl) **fuels** are *the oil, coal, and natural gas that are used to provide energy.* Burning fossil fuels releases toxic gases into the atmosphere that harm humans.

Acid Rain

Certain chemicals in gases, such as sulfur dioxides and nitrogen oxides, mix with moisture in the air to form **acid rain,** which is *rain that is more acidic than normal rain.* Over time, acid rain can harm plants and forests. It can also contaminate water supplies. Acid rain can even eat away at rock and stone.

Smog

Fossil fuels create other gases that are changed by heat and sunlight into **ozone,** *a gas made of three oxygen atoms.* In the upper atmosphere, ozone occurs naturally. It helps protect you from the sun's harmful rays. Closer to ground level, ozone mixes with other gases to form smog. **Smog** is *a yellow-brown haze that forms when sunlight reacts with air pollution.*

Ozone and smog can worsen existing health problems. For example, a person with bronchitis, asthma, or emphysema may have a very hard time breathing when smog is in the air. Many cities issue warnings on days when there is too much smog or ozone in the air.

On such days, people sensitive to smog or ozone should limit the time they spend outside.

You can **do your part** by using products that **won't cause** more *damage.*

Damage *to the* Ozone Layer

The **ozone layer** is *a shield above the earth's surface that protects living things from ultraviolet (UV) radiation.* In the 1970s, scientists discovered that the ozone layer was being damaged. This damage was caused by the chemicals used in aerosol cans, refrigerators, and air conditioners. It was also caused by emissions from automobiles. Without the ozone layer, people are more likely to develop skin cancer and eye damage.

Many countries are banning the use of the chemicals that damage the ozone layer. You can do your part by using products that will not cause more damage.

Global Warming

The trapping of heat by carbon dioxide and other gases in the air is known as the **greenhouse effect.** The greenhouse effect warms Earth which helps to support life. However, the release of carbon dioxide and other gases from burning fossil fuels increases the greenhouse effect. This may be the cause of **global warming,** or *a rise in Earth's temperatures.* Global warming can affect weather patterns as well as ocean water levels.

Increases in the greenhouse effect may cause global warming. *Describe what you can do to prevent the greenhouse effect.*

1. Light energy from the sun reaches the earth's lower atmosphere and is converted to heat.

2. A layer of carbon dioxide and other gases surrounding the earth traps the heat.

3. The surface of the earth and the lower atmosphere become warmer because of the trapped heat.

Pete Ryan/National Geographic Stock

WATER POLLUTION

MAIN IDEA Chemicals used on land are the primary source of water pollution.

Water is vital to all forms of life. However, wastes, chemicals, and other harmful substances pollute Earth's water. Water pollution is a widespread problem. Forty percent of all the nation's rivers, lakes, streams, and estuaries, or coastal areas, are too polluted to use for swimming, fishing, or drinking.

One type of pollution is sewage. Sewage is *human waste, garbage, detergents, and other household wastes washed down drains and toilets.* Sewage in the United States is treated. However, many countries do not properly treat water.

Chemicals used in industry also contribute to water pollution. Some enter the water from factories. Agriculture also contributes to water pollution. Oil spills from large tanker ships kill plants and animals and harm delicate habitats. Oil spills also run off into nearby lakes, rivers, and wetlands.

Water polluted with sewage can spread diseases. Eating shellfish from polluted water can cause hepatitis, a disease of the liver. Drinking water contaminated by metals such as lead or mercury can damage the liver, kidneys, and brain. It can also cause birth defects.

Pollution can affect your health as well as the health of every living thing around you. Before disposing of wastes, think about how they may affect the environment. What can you do to help protect the environment?

> ## Reading Check
>
> **DESCRIBE** *How could water pollution affect your health?*

Oil spills drop 37 million gallons of oil into the oceans yearly. Another 363 million gallons of oil reach oceans from oil changes done at home.

How much more oil comes from oil changes than from oil spills?

REVIEW

After You Read

1. **DEFINE** Define *fossil fuels*.
2. **RECALL** Name two sources of air pollution and two sources of water pollution.
3. **IDENTIFY** How is smog formed?

Thinking Critically

4. **EXPLAIN** How do fossil fuels contribute to global warming?
5. **ANALYZE** What is the difference between ozone in the upper atmosphere and ozone nearer to ground level?

Applying Health Skills

6. **ACCESSING INFORMATION** Use reliable sources to research the dangers of exposure to lead in water and explain how to avoid this potentially harmful substance. Report your findings to the class.

 Review

 Audio

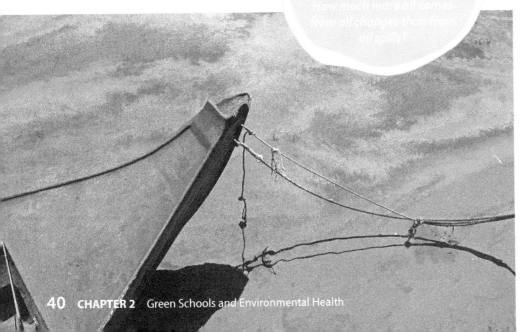

KEENPRESS/Getty Images

Preventing *and* Reducing Pollution

BIG IDEA You have the power to prevent and reduce pollution.

Before You Read

QUICK WRITE Make a list of actions you already take to reduce pollution.

 Video

As You Read

STUDY ORGANIZER Make the study organizer on page 55 to record the information presented in Lesson 2.

Vocabulary

› Environmental Protection Agency (EPA)
› Occupational Safety and Health Administration (OSHA)
› conservation
› biodegradable

 Audio

 Bilingual Glossary

©PhotoAlto

Fitness Zone

Increasing My Fitness I can increase my fitness by walking, riding a bicycle, skateboarding, or inline skating instead of riding in a vehicle. All of these activities are examples of aerobic exercise, which help keep my heart and lungs healthy. At the same time, I am reducing air pollution by not using fossil fuels!

KEEPING THE ENVIRONMENT CLEAN

MAIN IDEA The Environmental Protection Agency is a government agency committed to protecting the environment.

Lately, Brian has noticed how much trash his family throws away. A lot of the trash in the garbage seems to be plastic bottles and aluminum cans. He wonders if convincing his family to recycle would help reduce some of the waste.

We can all do our part to help reduce pollution. When we work together as a community, we can do even more. Governments around the world are committed to reducing and preventing pollution. In the United States, the Environmental Protection Agency (EPA) is *the governmental agency that is committed to protecting the environment.* The Occupational Safety and Health Administration (OSHA) is *a branch of the U.S. Department of Labor that protects American workers.*

It is the responsbility of OSHA to make sure that work environments are safe and free of hazardous materials. If a workplace requires the use of these materials, OSHA will help the company to store the hazardous materials safely.

Local governments play a role in protecting the environment too. Many local governments maintain air and water quality. Some methods they use are waste management strategies and controlling auto emissions.

We can all *do our part* to help reduce pollution.

Waste management is the disposal of wastes in a way that protects the health of the environment and the people.

Reading Check

EXPLAIN *What is the Environmental Protection Agency (EPA)?*

REDUCING AIR POLLUTION

MAIN IDEA Using alternative transportation, staying tobacco free, and planting trees can all help reduce air pollution.

Any time you use an electrical appliance, ride in a car, or run a lawn mower, you are burning fossil fuels to produce energy. You are also contributing to air pollution. Here are some strategies to help reduce air pollution in your community.

- **Walk or ride your bike.** When you ride a bike or walk rather than ride in a vehicle, you save fuel and reduce pollution. You can also get the benefit from some physical activity.

- **Use public transportation or carpool.** Carpooling, or taking a bus, train, or subway, cuts down on the number of cars producing exhaust fumes.

- **Stay tobacco free.** Tobacco smoke is not only unhealthy for people who smoke, it pollutes the air.

- **Plant trees and other plants.** Plants convert remove carbon dioxide from the air during photosynthesis, helping reduce the amount of carbon dioxide in the atmosphere.

When you use less of a resource, such as fossil fuels, you are practicing conservation. Conservation is *the saving of resources*. You can conserve energy resources in your own home for example, by turning off lights when you leave a room. When you conserve energy, you are also using less fossil fuels.

> **Reading Check**
>
> DESCRIBE *What can you do to promote cleaner air?*

Whenever you can, ride your bike rather than in a motor vehicle. It's better for the environment. *What health benefits do you get from riding a bike?*

Thinkstock Images/Comstock Images/Getty Images

REDUCING WATER POLLUTION

MAIN IDEA Picking up after pets, picking up litter, using environment-friendly products, and disposing of chemicals properly can all reduce water pollution.

We all need clean drinking water. Clean water is important for all plants and animals. The industries and farms that use water to produce the foods and beverages we eat and drink need clean water. We also need clean water for water recreation activities. To help keep water clean, follow these tips.

- Pick up pet waste from public areas to reduce toxic runoff.
- Use soaps, detergents, and cleaners that are biodegradable—*broken down easily in the environment.*
- Pick up any litter that is not hazardous.
- Dispose of chemicals properly and legally. Never pour them into a drain.
- Take hazardous waste materials to the appropriate collection sites.

Reading Check

LIST *What are two ways to reduce water pollution?*

The household products shown in this picture are all hazardous materials. *How do you safely dispose of hazardous wastes in your community?*

REVIEW

After You Read

1. **DEFINE** What is the *Environmental Protection Agency*?
2. **GIVE EXAMPLES** What can you do to reduce air pollution?
3. **LIST** Name three ways you can help keep water clean.

Thinking Critically

4. **INFER:** Why is it a good idea to turn off lights when you leave a room?
5. **ANALYZE** If conservation is a good idea, why do you think people might still need to be reminded to conserve resources?

Applying Health Skills

6. **ADVOCACY** Write and illustrate a comic book that encourages teens to conserve electricity and water. In your comic book, be sure to explain why conservation of these resources is important.

Review

Audio

Protecting *the* Environment

BIG IDEA There are many things that you can do to protect the environment.

PROTECTING NATURAL RESOURCES

MAIN IDEA Some resources, such as fossil fuels, are nonrenewable, meaning that they can be used only once.

Fossil fuels are natural materials known as non-renewable resources. **Nonrenewable resources** are *substances that cannot be replaced once they are used.* Fossil fuels such as oil, natural gas, or coal are extracted from underground. Once they are used, they cannot be replaced.

Conservation is a good way to **protect resources** such as water and trees.

Other resources are always being renewed. For example, the supply of freshwater is constantly being renewed through the water cycle. The water cycle refers to the natural movement of water through, around, and over the earth.

Even renewable resources, however, need to be protected. There is a limited amount of freshwater. Pollution makes freshwater more expensive because polluted water has to be cleaned before it is used. Trees are cut down to make paper and lumber. Removing too many trees upsets the balance of nature. By upsetting this balance, the lives of all living things are endangered. Conservation is a good way to protect resources such as water and trees.

> **Reading Check**

EXPLAIN *What is a nonrenewable resource?*

Conserving Water Resources

As a teen, you may wonder how you can conserve water resources. How can one person conserve water? You can do several things to conserve water both at home and elsewhere.

INSIDE THE HOUSE

- Avoid letting water run unnecessarily. For example, turn off the faucet while brushing your teeth, or washing your face.
- Wash clothes in warm or cold water, which uses less energy than hot water.
- Run the washing machine or dishwasher only when you have a full load, and use the short cycle when appropriate.

How can *one person* conserve water?

- If you have an older toilet, place a 1 liter bottle filled with water inside your toilet tank. This will reduce the amount of water used for flushing. Another option is to replace an older toilet with a newer model that requires less water per flush.
- Fix leaky faucets to avoid the loss of water throughout the day. Leaky faucets in a home can waste up to 10,000 gallons of water a year. That is enough water to fill a swimming pool.
- Install water-saving shower-heads or take shorter showers.

OUTSIDE THE HOUSE

- Turn the hose off when you are washing the car. Use the hose only for rinsing the car.
- Water lawns only when needed. Use soaker hoses for watering gardens. Avoid letting a sprinkler run while you are away from home.
- Garden with plants that conserve water.

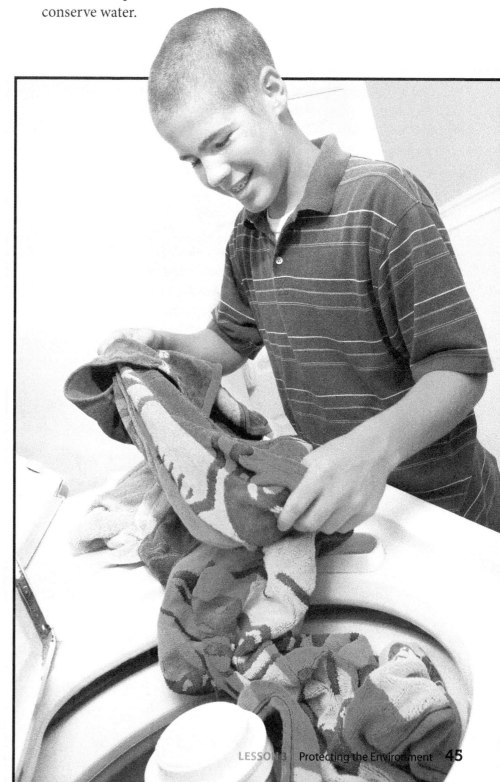

This teen is conserving water by doing a full load of laundry. *If water is a renewable resource why do we have to conserve it?*

ThinkStock/age fotostock

DEALING WITH WASTES

Land pollution results from littering. It also occurs as a result of the careless disposal of household and industrial garbage. Many of the items we use in daily life are made of plastic and metal. When they are thrown away, these materials take a long time to break down, if they ever do. This affects not only the soil but also the air and groundwater, or *water that collects under the earth's surface.*

Types *of* Wastes

The average U.S. citizen produces about four pounds of trash, or solid waste, daily. The solid waste produced by households and businesses usually ends up in landfills. A land-fill is *a huge specially designed pit where waste materials are dumped and buried.*

Landfills may have walls or linings so that water flowing through the landfill does not carry chemicals or other material into water supplies. In time, all landfills get filled up. When this happens, they are capped and sealed. A new landfill is made somewhere else.

Some wastes are hazardous to the health of all living things. Hazardous wastes are *Human-made liquid, solid, sludge or radioactive wastes that may endanger human health or the environment.* All hazardous wastes require special disposal. Hazardous wastes should be placed into a landfill. Some examples of hazardous wastes are dangerous industrial chemicals, asbestos, radioactive materials, as well as some medical wastes.

Hazardous substances from our homes include: motor oil, paint, insecticides, nail polish remover, antifreeze, bleach, and drain cleaner. Batteries, computers, and air conditioners also contain hazardous wastes.

Hazardous wastes are dangerous to the environment. To dispose of household hazardous waste, contact your local health department or environmental agency. They will explain how to get rid of it safely. Many communities have drop-off centers to collect household hazardous waste. Never put household hazardous wastes in the trash or pour chemicals down the drain.

>>> **Reading Check**

RECALL *What are two types of wastes?*

Even computers can harm the environment. *What other household products need to be disposed of as hazardous waste?*

Johner Royalty-Free/Getty Images

REDUCING, REUSING, AND RECYCLING

MAIN IDEA Precycling is reducing waste before it is used, and recycling conserves energy and natural resources.

REVIEW

Reducing wastes by _precycling—reducing waste before it occurs_—is one way to reduce the consumption of resources. Below are some basic guidelines for precycling:

- Buy products in packages made of glass, metal, or paper. It is possible to reuse or _recycle_ these materials, meaning _to change items in some way so that they can be used again._
- Carry purchases in your own reusable bags.
- Avoid using paper plates, plastic cups and utensils.
- Buy products in bulk to reduce packaging.

Reusing objects is another way to cut down on waste. For example, consider buying reusable food containers.

Reuse plastic grocery bags as trash bags. Donate unwanted clothes to charity rather than throwing the clothing out.

Recycling is _recovering and changing items so they can be used for other purposes._ Paper, aluminum, glass, plastics, and yard waste are the most commonly collected recycling materials. More and more people are becoming involved in recycling through drop-off centers and curbside programs.

As awareness of environmental health grows, people take a more active role in recycling. _What else can you infer from this graph?_

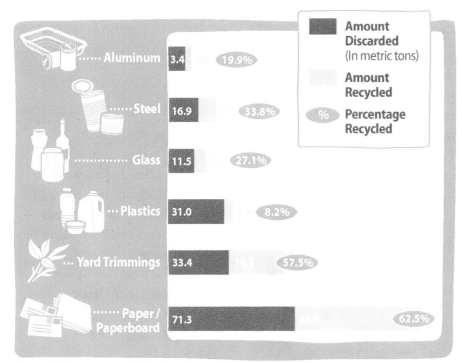

	Amount Discarded (In metric tons)	Amount Recycled	% Percentage Recycled
Aluminum	3.4		19.9%
Steel	16.9		33.8%
Glass	11.5		27.1%
Plastics	31.0		8.2%
Yard Trimmings	33.4		57.5%
Paper / Paperboard	71.3		62.5%

Source: U.S. Environmental Protection Agency, 2010.

After You Read

1. **DEFINE** What is a _nonrenewable resource_?
2. **DESCRIBE** Name five common products that contain hazardous materials that contribute to pollution.
3. **IDENTIFY** Name the three Rs and tell how they are related to your health.

Thinking Critically

4. **SYNTHESIZE** Explain why recycling and precycling are keys to a cleaner environment.
5. **ANALYZE** How does properly disposing of hazardous waste affect your environment as well as your personal health?

Applying Health Skills

6. **GOAL SETTING** Working with family members, evaluate your current approach to the three Rs and set specific goals to improve your household record for reducing, reusing, and recycling.

◉ Review

◉ Audio

Green Schools

BIG IDEA You can help your school become green.

Before You Read

QUICK WRITE What actions do you take at school to help protect the environment?

 Video

As You Read

STUDY ORGANIZER Make the study organizer on page 55 to record the information presented in Lesson 4.

Vocabulary

› green school

› pesticide

 Audio

🔤 Bilingual Glossary

WHAT IS A GREEN SCHOOL?

MAIN IDEA Green schools are environmentally friendly and provide a healthy environment for students.

Robert noticed a lot of paper was being thrown away in his school's garbage bins. He wondered if it might be a good idea to start a school recycling program. He asked his friends, other students, his teachers, and the school principal to join his program to help recycle the school's waste.

You may have heard the term *green* used to refer to programs or actions that are environmentally friendly. A **green school** is *one that is environmentally friendly in several different ways.* Green schools have made changes to conserve energy, water, and other resources. Their goal is to provide a healthy environment for students.

Green schools eliminate toxins such as mold, certain cleaning chemicals, and pesticides. A **pesticide** is a *product used on crops to kill insects and other pests.* Green schools make sustainable food choices, such as having a school garden, and reducing solid wastes. Solid wastes include food and paper.

Green schools have made changes to conserve energy, water, and other resources.

Green schools also work to educate students, parents, and the community about conserving resources and protecting the environment.

> **Reading Check**
>
> **EXPLAIN** *How can green schools provide a healthy environment for students?*

Myth vs. Fact

Myth: Changing our actions with regard to energy use at school doesn't really save energy.

Fact: When students and schools take steps to turn out lights in unoccupied rooms and turn off computers at night and on weekends, it can save energy and reduce energy bills by thousands of dollars per year.

LisaFx/age fotostock

BEING GREEN AT SCHOOL

MAIN IDEA You can protect the environment while at school.

Are you wondering what you can do to help protect the environment at school? The tips listed below may give you some ideas.

- **Don't litter.** Throw trash into trashcans and recycling bins. Pick up litter when you see it. Organize litter clean-up events in your community.
- **Conserve energy.** Walk, ride your bicycle, take the bus, or carpool. Turn off lights and other electronic equipment when they are not in use.
- **Conserve water.** Turn off the faucet while you wash your hands. Report leaking or dripping faucets or toilets to your teacher or principal.
- **Reduce solid waste.** Reuse paper by writing on both sides. Make double-sided copies or printouts. Pack a lunch from home in reusable containers and carry it in a reusable lunchbag.

Helping Your School Go Green

You can do many things to conserve resources. The following list contains steps you can take to help protect the environment.

- **Reduce exposure to chemicals.** Set up a program to properly dispose of hazardous wastes including batteries, fluorescent light bulbs, and electronic waste.
- **Start a recycling or composting program.** Recycle paper, plastic bottles, glass bottles, and aluminum cans. Build a compost pile so that food wastes from the kitchen can be composted.
- **Start a school garden.** Grow vegetables for your school's cafeteria. Have the kitchen incorporate food that you grow into lunches.
- **Start a group or club.** Create campaigns that explain how environmentally-friendly actions can be practiced.

> **>> Reading Check**
>
> **DESCRIBE** *Identify two actions to help protect the environment.* ■

Some schools provide bins for collecting different kinds of recyclable materials.

Photographer's Choice/Getty Images

REVIEW

>>> After You Read

1. **VOCABULARY** Define *green school.*
2. **DESCRIBE** What actions can you take to protect the environment at school?
3. **IDENTIFY** List three actions you can take to help your school be more green.

>>> Thinking Critically

4. **APPLY** Briefly describe how each of the following strategies help your school become more green and helps protect the environment: recycling paper and plastic products, planting a school garden.
5. **EVALUATE** Why is it important for schools to become actively involved in protecting the environment?

>>> Applying Health Skills

6. **COMMUNICATION SKILLS** Choose one action your school could take to become more green. Write a presentation that could be given at a school board meeting to advocate for this change. Include facts and statistics to support your request.

🔄 Review

🔊 Audio

Managing *the* Packaging

WHAT YOU WILL NEED

* small bag of potato chips
* wrapped slices of cheese
* video game (in original packaging)
* batteries (in original packaging)
* graph paper and pencil

WHAT YOU WILL DO

1 Work in small groups to create a graph.

2 Determine the unnecessary packaging of each of the four products. Rate them on a scale from 1 to 5, with 5 being the most unnecessary. Mark the product's rating on the graph's vertical (*y*) axis.

3 On a scale from 1 to 5, with 5 being the highest, rate the likelihood that a product could be recycled or reused. Mark the product's rating on the horizontal (*x*) axis.

4 Draw a horizontal line out from the product's packaging rating. Draw a vertical line up from the product's recycling rating. Where the lines meet, write the name of the product.

Packaging can be useful when it protects a product. Packaging can also be wasteful. Unnecessary packaging uses up the Earth's resources and can harm the environment when discarded.

©Comstock Images/Getty Images

WRAPPING IT UP

What did you consider before deciding where to place the product on the graph? Where on the graph do you find the objects that are the most environment-friendly? Where are the least environment-friendly objects?

READING REVIEW

FOLDABLES and Other Study Aids

Take out the Foldable® that you created for Lesson 1 and any study organizers that you created for Lessons 2-4. Find a partner and quiz each other using these study aids.

LESSON 1 Pollution and Health

BIG IDEA Pollution harms the environment and your health, and is often ugly.

- Pollution is made up of dirty or harmful substances in the environment.
- Burning fossil fuels such as coal, oil, and natural gas pollutes the air.
- Chemicals used on land are the primary source of water pollution.

LESSON 2 Preventing and Reducing Pollution

BIG IDEA You have the power to prevent and reduce pollution.

- The Environmental Protection Agency is a government agency committed to protecting the environment.
- Using alternative transportation, staying tobacco free, and planting trees can all help reduce air pollution.
- Picking up after pets, picking up litter, using environment-friendly products, and disposing of chemicals properly can all reduce water pollution.

LESSON 3 Protecting the Environment

BIG IDEA There are many things that you can do to protect the environment.

- Some resources, such as fossil fuels, are nonrenewable, meaning that they can be used only once.
- Recycling and conservation have a positive impact on the environment.
- Precycling is reducing waste before it is used, and recycling conserves energy and natural resources.

LESSON 4 Green Schools

BIG IDEA You can help your school become green.

- Green schools are environmentally friendly and provide a healthy environment for students.
- You can protect the environment while at school.

 Review

 Web Quest

ASSESSMENT

Reviewing Vocabulary *and* Main Ideas

- pollution
- acid rain
- ozone
- sewage
- Environmental Protection Agency
- conservation
- biodegradable
- Occupational Safety and Health Administration

On a sheet of paper, write the numbers 1–8. After each number, write the term from the list that best completes each statement.

LESSON 1 Pollution and Health

1. _____ can carry pathogens that cause disease.

2. Up in the atmosphere, _____ protects people from UV rays; closer to earth, it is part of smog.

3. Dirty or harmful substances in the environment are _____.

4. _____ can ruin forests and even eat away at stone.

LESSON 2 Preventing and Reducing Pollution

5. Waste that is _____ can easily break down in the environment.

6. _____ is the saving of resources.

7. The _____ is a governmental agency that is committed to protecting the environment.

8. A branch of the U.S. Department of Labor that protects workers is called _____.

On a sheet of paper, write the numbers 9–14. Write *True* or *False* for each statement below. If the statement is false, change the underlined word or phrase to make it true.

LESSON 3 Protecting the Environment

9. Buying a food container that can be used many times to store food is an example of <u>recycling</u>.

10. Oil, natural gas, and coal are <u>renewable</u> resources.

11. Using fluorescent light bulbs can <u>save</u> electricity.

12. Conservation is the <u>wasting</u> of resources.

LESSON 4 Green Schools

13. A green school is environmentally <u>unfriendly</u>.

14. <u>Pesticides</u> are toxic chemicals used to kill insects.

✔ eAssessment

Using complete sentences, answer the following questions on a sheet of paper.

 Thinking **Critically**

15. INFER What do you think is meant by the saying "We all live downstream"?

16. INTERPRET A volcanic eruption can send tons of smoke and ash into the air. Do volcanoes pollute? Explain your answer.

 Write **About It**

17. OPINION Write a short essay explaining why you think some products have more packaging than necessary. Include ideas as to how reducing excess packaging could help the environment.

STANDARDIZED TEST PRACTICE

Reading

Read the passage below and then answer the questions that follow.

Think about how often you throw away plastic, such as milk cartons or soda bottles. Using and then throwing away plastic causes landfills to fill up quickly. In the past, objects made out of wood, paper, cotton, or wool would biodegrade fairly easily. These objects broke down naturally over time. However, plastic items do not break down. That means plastic wastes must be stored in a landfill. Recently, scientists have discovered a way to make a sturdy, durable plastic that biodegrades when buried in dirt. Scientists are hopeful that using biodegradable plastic will help reduce the amount of waste buried in landfills.

1. What is the main point of the passage?
   A. Life was better years ago.
   B. Wood and paper are biodegradable.
   C. Biodegradable plastic will reduce the waste in landfills.
   D. Throwing away more plastic will actually reduce the waste in landfills.

2. What does *durable* mean in this sentence? Recently, scientists have discovered a way to make a sturdy, durable plastic that biodegrades when buried in dirt.
   A. weak
   B. flexible
   C. tough
   D. large

CHAPTER 1

Foldables®

Make this Foldable® to help you organize what you learn in Lesson 1 about safety.

1 Begin with three plain sheets of 8 ½" x 11" paper. Place the sheets ½" apart.

3 Crease the paper to hold the tabs in place and staple along the fold.

2 Roll up the bottom edges, stopping them ½" from the top edges. This makes all tabs the same size.

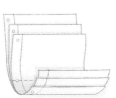

Record information from each lesson in the chapter about safety under each appropriate tab.

Study Organizers

Use the following study organizers to record the information presented in Lessons 2–6.

Lesson 2:
Two-Column Chart

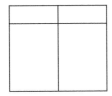

Lesson 3:
Outline

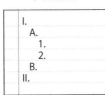

Lesson 4:
Three-Column Chart

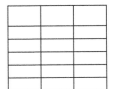

Lesson 5:
K-W-L Chart

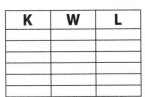

Lesson 6:
Index Cards

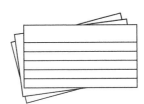

CHAPTER 2

Foldables®

Make this Foldable® to help you organize what you learn in Lesson 1 about environmental health.

 Begin with a plain sheet 8 ½" x 11" paper from top to bottom, leaving a 2" tab at the bottom.

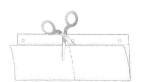

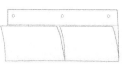 Unfold the paper once. Cut along the center fold line of the top layer only. This makes two tabs.

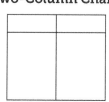 Fold in half from side to side.

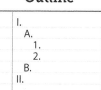

Under the appropriate tab, take notes on the causes and effects of pollution.

Study Organizers

Use the following study organizers to record the information presented in Lessons 2–4.

Lesson 2: Two-Column Chart	Lesson 3: Outline	Lesson 4: Flow Chart

	I.
	  A.
	    1.
	    2.
	  B.
	II.
		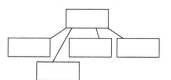

Glossary/Glosario

English

Abdominal thrust Quick inward and upward pull into the diaphragm to force an obstruction out of the airway.

Abstinence (AB stuh nuhns) The conscious, active choice not to participate in high-risk behaviors.

Accident Any event that was not intended to happen.

Accident chain A series of events that include a situation, an unsafe habit, and an unsafe action.

Accidental injuries Injuries resulting from an accident.

Acid rain Rain that is more acidic than normal rain.

Advocacy Taking action in support of a cause.

Aftershocks Smaller earthquakes as the earth readjusts after the main earthquake.

Attitude (AT ih tood) Feelings and beliefs.

Biodegradable (by oh di GRAY duh buhl) Easily broken down in the environment.

Blizzard A very heavy snowstorm with winds up to 45 miles per hour.

Cardiopulmonary resuscitation (CPR) A first-aid procedure to restore breathing and circulation.

Communication The exchange of information through the use of words or actions.

Conflict resolution A life skill that involves solving a disagreement in a way that satisfies both sides.

Conservation The saving of resources.

Cultural background The beliefs, customs, and traditions of a specific group of people.

Culture the collected beliefs, customs, and behaviors of a group

Cumulative (KYOO myuh luh tiv) risk When one risk factor adds to another to increase danger.

Español

presión abdominal Presión rápida, hacia adentro y arriba sobre el diafragma, para desalojar un objeto que bloquea la vía respiratoria de una persona.

abstinencia Opción activa y conciente de no participar en comportamientos de alto riesgo.

accidente Suceso que ocurre de manera no intencional.

accidente en cadena Serie de sucesos que incluye una situación, un hábito peligroso y un acto peligroso.

lesiones accidentales Lesiones que resultan de un accidente.

lluvia ácida Lluvia que es más ácida de lo normal.

promoción Actuar en apoyo de una causa.

réplica sísmica Temblores mas pequeños que ocurren mientras la tierra se reajusta después de un terremoto principal.

actitud Sentimientos y creencias.

biodegradable Que se descompone fácilmente en el medio ambiente.

ventisca Tormenta de nieve fuerte, con vientos que llegan a 45 millas por hora.

resucitación cardiopulmonar Procedimiento de primeros auxilios para restaurar la respiración y la circulación de la sangre.

comunicación Intercambio de información a través del uso de palabras y acciones.

resolución de un conflicto Habilidad que implica el hecho de resolver un desacuerdo satisfaciendo a los dos lados.

conservación Protección de los recursos naturales.

base cultural Creencias, costumbres y tradiciones de un grupo especifico de personas.

cultura Colección de creencias, costumbres y comportamientos de un grupo.

riesgo acumulativo Cuando un factor riesgoso se suma a otro e incrementa el peligro.

English

Español

Decision making The process of making a choice or solving a problem.

tomar decisiones Proceso de hacer una selección o de resolver un problema.

Defensive driving Watching out for other people on the road and anticipating unsafe acts.

conducir de manera defensiva Estar atento a las otras personas en la carretera y anticipar acciones peligrosas.

Dislocation A major injury that happens when a bone is forced from its normal position within a joint.

dislocación Daño mayor que ocurre cuando un hueso es forzado fuera de lugar en la articulación.

Earthquake A shifting of the earth's plates resulting in a shaking of the earth's surface.

terremoto Cambio de las placas terrestres que hace que la superficie terrestre tiemble.

Electrical overload A dangerous situation in which too much electric current flows along a single circuit.

sobrecarga eléctrica Situación peligrosa en que demasiada corriente eléctrica fluye a través de un solo circuito.

Environment (en VY ruhn muhnt) All the living and nonliving things around you.

medio Todas las cosas vivas y no vivas que te rodean.

Environmental Protection Agency (EPA) An agency of the U.S. government that is dedicated to protecting the environment.

Agencia de Protección Agencia del gobierno de Estados Unidos a cargo de la protección del medio ambiente.

Fire extinguisher A device that sprays chemicals that put out fires.

extintor de fuego Aparato que rocia productos químicos que apagan fuegos.

First aid The immediate care given to someone who becomes injured or ill until regular medical care can be provided.

primeros auxilios Cuidado inmediato que se da a una persona herida o enferma hasta que sea posible proporcionarle ayuda médica normal.

Flammable Substances that catch fire easily.

inflamable Sustancias que se encienden fácilmente.

Fossil (FAH suhl) fuels The oil, coal, and natural gas that are used to provide energy.

combustible fósil Petróleo, carbón y gas natural que se usan para proporcionar energía.

Fracture A break in a bone.

fractura Rotura de un hueso.

Fraud A calculated effort to trick or fool others.

fraude Esfuerzo calculado para engañar a otros.

Frostbite freezing of the skin

congelación Congelamiento de la piel.

Global warming A rise in the earth's temperatures.

calentamiento del planeta Aumento en las temperaturas de la Tierra.

Goal setting The process of working toward something you want to accomplish.

establecer metas Proceso de esforzarte para lograr algo que quieres.

Greenhouse effect The trapping of heat by carbon dioxide and other gases in the air.

efecto invernadero Retención del calor por la presencia de dióxido de carbono y otros gases en el aire.

Green School A school that is environmentally-friendly in several different ways.

escuela verde Una escuela que es respetuoso con el medio ambiente de varias maneras diferentes.

Groundwater Water that collects under the earth's surface.

agua subterránea Agua acumulada debajo de la superficie de la tierra.

Glossary/Glosario

English

Hazard Potential source of danger.

Hazardous wastes Human-made liquid, solid, sludge or radioactive wastes that may endanger human health or the environment.

Health The combination of physical, mental/emotional, and social well-being.

Health care any services provided to individuals or communities that promote, maintain, or restore health

Health care system All the medical care available to a nation's people, the way they receive the care, and the way the care is paid for.

Health fraud The selling of products or services to prevent diseases or cure health problems which have not been scientifically proven safe or effective for such purposes.

Health insurance A plan in which a person pays a set fee to an insurance company in return for the company's agreement to pay some or all medical expenses when needed.

Health maintenance organization (HMO) A health insurance plan that contracts with selected physicians and specialists to provide medical services.

Health skills skills that help you become and stay healthy

Heredity (huh RED I tee) The passing of traits from parents to their biological children.

Hospice care Care provided to the terminally ill that focuses on comfort, not cure.

Hurricane A strong windstorm with driving rain that forms over the sea.

Hypothermia (hy poh THER mee uh) A sudden and dangerous drop in body temperature.

Landfill Huge specially designed pit where waste materials are dumped and buried.

Lifestyle factors Behaviors and habits that help determine a person's level of health.

Long-term goal A goal that you plan to reach over an extended period of time.

Español

peligro Fuente posible de peligro.

desperdicios peligrosos Líquidos, sólidos, sedimentos, o desperdicios radiactivos producidos por humanos que ponen en peligro la salud humana o el medio ambiente.

salud Combinación de bienestar físico, mental/emocional y social.

cuidado medico Cualquier servicio proporcionado a individuos o comunidades que promueve, mantiene y les hace recobrar la salud.

sistema de cuidado de la salud Servicios médicos disponibles para a la gente de una nación y las formas en las cuales estos son pagados.

fraude médico Venta de productos o servicios para prevenir enfermedades o curar problemas de salud que no han sido aprobados científicamente o hechos efectivos para ese uso.

seguro médico Plan en el que una persona paga una cantidad fija a una compañía de seguros que acuerda cubrir parte o la totalidad de los gastos médicos.

organización para el mantenimiento de la salud Plan de seguro de salud que contrata a ciertos médicos y especialistas para dar servicios médicos.

habilidades de salud Habilidades que ayudan a ser y mantenerte saludable.

herencia Transferencia de características de los padres biológicos a sus hijos.

asistencia para enfermos Asistencia para personas con enfermedades incurables que apunta a brindar comodidad, no a la cura.

huracán Tormenta de vientos y lluvia torrencial que se origina en alta mar.

hipotermia Descenso rápido y peligroso de la temperatura del cuerpo.

terraplén sanitario Pozo enorme con diseño específico donde se arrojan y se entierran desechos.

factores del estilo de vida Conductas y hábitos que ayudan a determinar el nivel de salud de una persona.

meta a largo plazo Objetivo que planeas alcanzar en un largo periodo de tiempo.

English

Español

Managed care A health insurance plan that saves money by encouraging patients and providers to select less costly forms of care.

cuidado controlado Plan de seguro médico que ahorra dinero al limitar la selección de doctores de las personas.

Media Various methods for communicating information.

medios de difusión Diversos métodos de comunicar información.

Mind-body connection How your emotions affect your physical and overall health and how your overall health affects your emotions.

conexión de la mente con el cuerpo Forma en la cual tus emociones afectan tu salud física y general, y como tu salud general afecta tus emociones.

Natural disaster an event caused by nature that result in widespread damage, destruction, and loss

desastre natural Evento causado por la naturaleza que resulta en daños extensos, destrucción y pérdida.

Nonrenewable resources Substances that cannot be replaced once they are used.

recursos no renovables Sustancias que no se pueden reemplazar después de usarse.

Occupational Safety and Health Administration (OSHA) A branch of the U.S. Department of Labor that protects American workers.

Administración de Salud y Seguridad Ocupacional Rama del Ministerio del Trabajo que protege la seguridad de los trabajadores estadounidenses.

Ozone (OH zohn) A gas made of three oxygen atoms.

ozono Gas hecho de tres átomos de oxígeno.

Ozone layer A shield above the earth's surface that protects living things from ultraviolet (UV) radiation.

capa de ozono Capa protectora sobre la superficie de la Tierra que protege a los seres vivos de la radiación ultravioleta.

Pedestrian A person who travels on foot.

peatón Persona que se traslada a pie.

Peers People close to you in age who are a lot like you.

compañeros Personas de tu grupo de edad que se parecen a ti de muchas maneras.

Pesticide Product used on crops to kill insects and other pests.

pesticida Producto que se usa en las cosechas para matar insectos y otras plagas.

Pollute (puh LOOT) to make unfit or harmful for living things

contaminar Hacer lo impropio o dañoso para las cosas vivientes.

Pollution Dirty or harmful substances in the environment.

contaminación Sustancias sucias o dañinas en el medio ambiente.

Precautions Planned actions taken before an event to increase the chances of a safe outcome.

precauciones Acciones planeadas que son tomadas antes de un evento para incrementar la seguridad.

Precycling Reducing waste before it occurs.

preciclaje Proceso de reducir los desechos antes de que se produzcan.

Prevention Taking steps to avoid something.

prevención Tomar pasos para evitar algo.

Preventive care Steps taken to keep disease or injury from happening or getting worse.

cuidado preventivo Medidas que se toman para evitar que ocurran enfermedades o daños o que empeoren.

Primary care provider Health care professional who provides checkups and general care.

profesional médico principal Profesional de la salud que proporciona exámenes médicos y cuidado general.

Glossary/Glosario

English

Español

Recycle To change items in some way so that they can be used again.

reciclar Cambiar un objeto de alguna manera para que se pueda volver a usar.

Recycling recovering and changing items so they can be used for other purposes

reciclaje Recuperar y cambiar un objeto para usarlo con otro propósito.

Refusal skills Strategies that help you say no effectively.

habilidades de rechazo Estrategias que ayudan a decir no efectivamente.

Reliable Trustworthy and dependable.

confiable Confiable y seguro.

Rescue breathing A first-aid procedure where someone forces air into the lungs of a person who cannot breathe on his or her own.

respiración de rescate Procedimiento de primeros auxilios en el que una persona llena de aire los pulmones de una persona que no está respirando.

Risk The chance that something harmful may happen to your health and wellness.

riesgo Posibilidad de que algo dañino pueda ocurrir en tu salud y bienestar.

Risk behavior An action or behavior that might cause injury or harm to you or others.

conducta arriesgada Acto o conducta que puede causarte daño o perjudicarte a ti o a otros.

Safety conscious Being aware that safety is important and careful to act in a safe manner.

consciente de la seguridad Que se da cuenta de la importancia de la seguridad y actúa con cuidado.

Sewage Human waste, garbage, detergents, and other household wastes washed down drains and toilets.

aguas cloacales Basura, detergentes y otros desechos caseros que se llevan las tuberías de desagüe.

Short-term goal A goal that you can achieve in a short length of time.

meta a corto plazo Meta que uno puede alcanzar dentro de un breve periodo de tiempo.

Smog Yellow-brown haze that forms when sunlight reacts with air pollution.

smog Neblina de color amarillo-café que se forma cuando la luz solar reacciona con la contaminación del aire.

Smoke alarm A device that sounds an alarm when it senses smoke.

alarma contra incendios Aparato que hace sonar una alarma cuando detecta humo.

Specialist (SPEH shuh list) Health care professional trained to treat a special category of patients or specific health problems.

especialista Profesional del cuidado de la salud que está capacitado para tratar una categoría especial de pacientes o un problema de salud específico.

Stress The body's response to real or imagined dangers or other life events.

estrés Reacción del cuerpo hacia peligros reales o imaginarios u otros eventos en la vida.

English	Español
	T
Tornado A whirling, funnel-shaped windstorm that drops from storm clouds to the ground.	**tornado** Tormenta en forma de torbellino, que gira en grandes círculos y que cae del cielo a la tierra.
	U
Universal precautions Actions taken to prevent the spread of disease by treating all blood as if it were contaminated.	**precauciones universales** Medidas para prevenir la propagación de enfermedades al tratar toda la sangre como si estuviera contaminada.
	V
Values The beliefs that guide the way a person lives.	**valores** Creencias que guían la forma en la cual vive una persona.
	W
Weather emergency A dangerous situation brought on by changes in the atmosphere.	**emergencia meteorológica** Situación peligrosa debido a cambios en la atmósfera.
Wellness A state of well-being or balanced health over a long period of time.	**bienestar** Mantener una salud balanceada por un largo período de tiempo.

Index

Index

Index

water, 40, 44
Practicing healthful behaviors
    creating an emergency supplies kit, 21
    as health skill, xvii
Precautions, 17
Precycling, 47
Predators, Internet, 18
Prevention. *See also* Safety
    defined, xiv
    practicing healthful behaviors for, xvii
Preventive care, xxv
P.R.I.C.E. method, 28
Privacy settings, 18
Private health care plans, xxvii
Protective gear, viii, xiii
Public transportation, 42

R

Realistic goals, xxiii
Recycling, 47, 49
Reducing wastes, 47, 49
Refusal skills, xx
    defined, xx
    and gun safety, 9
Relationships, for social health, ix
Reliable, xviii
Reliable sources of information, xviii
Renewable resources, 44
Rescue breathing, 26
Responsibility
    and accident prevention, 4
    for personal safety, 16
Reusing objects, 47
Risk behaviors, xiii–xiv
Risk factors for health, xi–xii
    culture, xii
    environment, xi
    heredity, xi
    media, xii
Risk(s)
    consequences of taking, xiv
    cumulative, xiv
    defined, xiii
    reducing, xiv–xv
Road safety, 11–12
Rules, 9
Running, F4F-6

S

Safety, 2–30
    accidents, 4–5
    fire safety, 8–9
    first aid, 23–29
    in the home, 6–9
    home emergency kit for, 30
    in natural disasters, 21–22
    online, 17–18
    outdoors, 13–15
    personal, 16–17
    on the road, 11–12
    at school, 10
    in weather emergencies, 19–20
Safety gear, 9
Safety-consciousness, 4
School gardens, 49
Schools
    green, 48–49
    safety at, 10
Scooter safety, 12
Second-degree burns, 27
Self-management skills, xvii–xviii
    decision making, xviii, xxi–xxii
    goal setting, xviii, xxiii
    practicing healthful behaviors, xvii
    stress management, xvii
Settings, health care, xxvi–xxvii
Severe bleeding, first aid for, 27
Severe weather bulletins, 19
Sewage, 40
Short-term goals, xxiii
Skateboarding safety, 12
Skating safety, 12
Sleep, for health, viii
Smog, 39
Smoke alarms, 6, 9
Smoking safety, 8
Social environment, xi
Social health, ix, xvii
Specialists, health care, xxv
Sports, preparing for, F4F-8
Sprains, first aid for, 28
Sprinkler systems, 6
Staircase safety, 7
Storm bulletins, 19
Strength, muscle, F4F-3
Stress, xvii

FLIP 4 FITNESS

Flip for Fitness is for everyone. Non-athletes who avoid joining organized sports can develop a personal fitness plan to stay in shape. Even athletes can use some of the tips to cross train for their favorite sport.

Planning a Routine

Flip for Fitness helps you plan a fitness routine that helps your body slowly adjust to activity. Over time, you will increase both the length of time you spend and the number of times that you are physically active each week. Teens should aim to get at least one hour of physical activity each day. These periods of physical activity can be divided into shorter segments, such as three 20 minute segments each day. Exercise includes any physical activity, such as completing a fitness plan, playing individual or group sports, or even helping clean at home. The key is to keep your body moving.

Before You Start Exercising

Every activity session should begin with a warm-up to prepare your body for exercise. Warm-ups raise your body temperature and get your muscles ready for physical activity. Easy warm-up activities include walking, marching, and jogging, as well as basic calisthenics or stretches. As you increase the time you spend doing a fitness activity, you should increase the time you spend warming up. Check the Sample Physical Fitness Plan in Teen Health in Connect Ed.

Alistair Berg/Digital Vision/Getty Images

Fitness Information *and* Resources

Fitness Apps *and* Other Resources

»  USDA's MyPlate The MyPlate Super Tracker is a free online fitness and diet tracker. To review the tracker, go online to https://www.choosemyplate.gov and search for "Super Tracker".

» Additionally, organizations such as the American Heart Association and KidsHealth provide resources on developing walking programs. The online addresses are: http://startwalkingnow.org and http://kidshealth.org.

» Finally, smartphone and tablet users can download several nutrition and fitness tracking apps. Many are free of charge. Use the terms "fitness", "exercise", or "workout" when searching for apps.

Accessing Information

» The Teen Health online program includes resources to develop your own fitness plan. Check out the Fitness Zone resources in ConnectEd.

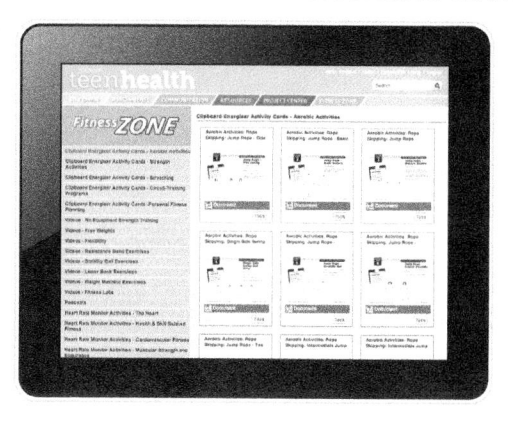

» The Centers for Disease Control and Prevention's, Body & Mind (BAM) web site also provide fitness information. The online address is: http://www.bam.gov. Search for "physical activity" or "activity cards."

Safety Tips

On the following pages, you'll find fitness activities for groups or individuals. Each activity includes information on what you'll need, how to start, and how to stay safe. Safety is the most important factor.

⚠ Always be aware of where you are and don't take any unnecessary chances.

⚠ Obey the rules of the road while riding your bicycle, avoid unsafe areas, and use the proper safety equipment when working out.

⚠ Finally, remember to drink water and to rest between exercise sessions.

 Elements *of* Fitness

When developing a fitness plan, it's helpful to have a goal. Maybe your goal is to comfortably ride your bike to school each day or maybe you want to complete the Tour de France in the future. Regardless of the reasons why you develop a fitness plan, focusing on the five elements of fitness will help you achieve overall physical fitness. The five elements are:

1 Cardiovascular Endurance
The ability of the heart and lungs to function efficiently over time without getting tired. Familiar examples are jogging, walking, bike riding, and swimming.

2 Muscle Endurance
The ability of a muscle or a group of muscles to work non-stop without getting tired. Many activities that build cardiovascular endurance also build muscular endurance, such as jogging, walking, and bike riding.

3 Muscle Strength
The ability of the muscle to produce force during an activity. Activities that can help build muscle strength include push-ups, pull-ups, lifting weights, and running stairs.

4 Flexibility
The ability to move a body part freely, without pain. Improve your flexibility by stretching gently before and after exercise.

5 Body Composition
The amount of body fat a person has compared with the amount of lean mass, which is bone, muscle, and fluid. A healthy body is made up of more lean mass and less body fat. Body composition is a result of diet, exercise, and heredity.

Fitness Circuit

Are you looking for a quick workout that will develop endurance, strength, and flexibility? A Fitness Circuit may be just what you need. Many public parks have Fitness Circuits (sometimes called Par Courses) with exercise stations located throughout a park. You walk or run between stations as part of your workout. A fitness circuit can also be created in your backyard or even a basement.

What Will I Need?

» Access to a public park or a home-made Fitness Circuit course.

» Comfortable workout clothes that wick away perspiration.

» Athletic shoes.

» Stopwatch (optional).

» Jump rope, dumbbells, exercise bands, or check out the Fitness Zone Clipboard Energizer Activity Cards, Circuit Training for ideas.

How Do I Start?

» In the park, read the instructions at each exercise station and perform the exercises as shown. Use the correct form. Try to do as many repetitions as you can for 30 seconds.

» After you finish the exercise, walk or run to the next station and complete that exercise.

» Check your heart rate to see how intensely you exercised at the end of the Fitness Circuit.

» Every month or so, consider adding a new exercise.

How Can I Stay Safe?

» Be alert to your surroundings in a public park. It is best to have a friend with you. It's also more fun to exercise with a friend.

» At home, leave enough room between stations to allow you to move and exercise freely. Avoid clutter in your exercise area.

» Perform the exercises correctly and at your own pace.

Walking

Walking is more than just a way to get from one place to another. It's also a great physical activity. By walking for as little as 30 minutes each day you can reduce your risk of heart disease, manage your weight, and even reduce stress. Walking requires very little equipment and you can do it almost anywhere. More good news: Walking is also something you can do by yourself or with friends and family.

Colin Hawkins/Cultura/Getty Images

What Will I Need?

» Running or walking shoes. Many athletic shoe stores sell both.

» Loose comfortable clothes that wick away perspiration. Layering is also a good idea. Consider adding a hat, sunglasses, and sunscreen if needed.

» Stopwatch and water bottle unless there are water fountains on your route.

» A pedometer or GPS to track your distance.

How Do I Start?

» Five minutes of easy stretching.

» Walk upright with good posture. Do not exaggerate your stride or swing your arms across your body.

» Build your time and distance slowly. One mile or 20 minutes every other day may be enough for the first couple weeks. Eventually you will want to walk at least 30-60 minutes five days a week.

How Can I Stay Safe?

» Let your parents know where you will be walking and how long you will be gone.

» Avoid wearing headphones if by yourself or if walking on a road or street.

Running *or* Jogging

Running or jogging is one of the best all-around fitness activities. Running uses the large muscles of the legs thereby burning lots of calories and also gives your heart and lungs a good workout in a shorter amount of time. Running also helps get you into condition to play team sports like basketball, football, or soccer. More good news is that running can be done on your schedule although it's also fun to run with a friend or two.

What Will I Need?

» A good pair of running shoes. Ask your Physical Education teacher or an employee at a specialist running shop to help you choose the right pair.

» Socks made of cotton or another type of material that wicks away perspiration.

» Bright colored or reflective clothing and shoes.

» A stopwatch or watch with a second sweep to time your runs or track your distance.

» Optional equipment might include a jacket or other layer depending on the weather, sunscreen, and sunglasses.

How Do I Start?

Your ultimate goal is to run at least 20 to 30 minutes at least 3 days a week. Use the training schedule shown below. Start by walking and gradually increasing the amount of time you run during each exercise session. Starting slowly will help your muscles and tendons adjust to the increased work load. Try spacing the three runs over an entire week so that you have one day in-between runs to recover.

How Can I Stay Safe?

» Use the correct equipment for the sport you have chosen.

» Running on a track, treadmill, or in a park with level ground will help you avoid foot or ankle injuries.

» Avoid running on the road, especially at night.

» Avoid wearing headphones unless you are on a track, treadmill, or another safe place. Safety experts agree that headphones can distract you from being alert to your surroundings.

Here is a plan to get you started as a runner:

» Start each run with a brisk 3-5 minute walk to warm-up.

» Take some time to slowly stretch the muscles and areas of the body involved in running. Avoid "bouncing" when stretching or trying to force a muscle or tendon to stretch when you start to feel tightness.

» Begin slowly and gradually increase your distance and speed. A good plan for the first several weeks is to alternate walking with easy running. The running plan included in this section can give you some tips on how to train for a 5K run.

» Use the "talk test." Can you talk in complete sentences during your training runs? If not, you are running too fast.

Training Schedule

M W F	Split Schedule	Duration
Week 1	Brisk 5 min. walk Walk: 60 - 90 seconds Run: 60 seconds	Repeat for 20 min.
Week 2 and 3	Brisk 5 min. walk Walk: 60 seconds Run: 60 - 90 seconds	Repeat for 20 min.
Week 4	Brisk 5 min. walk Walk: 60 seconds Run: 3 - 5 minutes	Repeat for 20 min.
Week 5+	Brisk 5 min. walk Run: 20 to 30 minutes	

Preparing *for* Sports *and* Other Activities

Do you want to play a sport? If so, think about developing a fitness plan for that sport. Some of the questions to ask yourself are: Does the sport require anaerobic activity, like running and jumping hurdles? Does the sport require aerobic fitness, like cross-country running? Other sports, such as football and track require muscular strength. Sports like basketball require special skills like dribbling, passing, and shot making. A workout plan for that sport will help you get into shape before organized practice and competition begins.

What Will I Need?

Each sport has different equipment requirements. Talk to a coach or physical education teacher about how to get ready for your sport. You can also conduct online research to learn what type of equipment you will need, such as:

» Proper footwear and workout clothes for a specific sport.

» What facilities are available for training and practice, such as a running track, tennis court, football or soccer field, or other safe open area.

» Where you can access weights and others form of resistance training as part of your training.

How Do I Start?

Now that your research is done, you can create your fitness plan. Include the type of exercises you will do each training day.

» Include a warm-up in your plan.

» List the duration of time that you will work out.

» Plan to exercise 3–5 days a week doing at least one kind of exercise each day. Remember to include stretching before every workout.

How Can I Stay Safe?

» Get instruction on how to use free weights and machines

» Make sure you start every activity with a warm-up.

» Ease into your fitness plan gradually so you do not pull a muscle or do too much too soon.

» Practice good nutrition and drink plenty of water to stay hydrated.

Interval Training

Getting fit takes time. One method, interval training, can show improvement in two weeks or less. Interval training consists of a mix of activities. First you do a few minutes of intense exercise. Next, you do easier, less-intense activity that enables your body to recover. Interval training can improve your cardiovascular endurance. It also helps develop speed and quickness.

Intervals are typically done as part of a running program. Not everyone wants to be a runner though. Intervals can also be done riding a bicycle or while swimming. On a bicycle, alternate fast pedaling with easier riding. In a pool, swim two fast laps followed by slower, easier laps.

What Will I Need?

» A running track or other flat area with marked distances like a football or soccer field.

» If at a park, 5–8 cones or flags to mark off distances of 30 to 100 yards.

» A training partner to help you push yourself (optional).

How Do I Start?

» After warming up, alternate brisk walking (or easy jogging). On a football field or track, walk 30 yards, jog 30 yards, and then run at a fast pace for 30 yards. Rest for one minute and repeat this circuit several times. If at a park, use cones or flags to mark off similar distances.

» Accelerate gradually into the faster strides so you stay loose and feel in control of the pace.

» If possible, alternate running up stadium steps instead of fast running on a track. This will help your coordination as well as your speed. Running uphill in a park would have similar benefits.

How Can I Stay Safe?

» Interval training works the heart and lungs. For this reason, a workout using interval training should be done only once or twice a week with a day off between workouts.

» Check with your doctor first. If you have any medical condition like high blood pressure or asthma, ask your doctor if interval training is safe for you.